VEDANTA PHILOSOPHY

RAJA YOGA

VEDANTA PHILOSOPHY

RAJA YOGA

BEING LECTURES BY THE

SWAMI VIVEKANANDA

WITH PATANJALI'S APHORISMS, COMMENTARIES

AND A GLOSSARY OF TERMS

GYAN

Published by

Gyan Publishing House
5, Ansari Road
Daryaganj, New Delhi-110002
Phone: 011-47034999, 9811692060
E-mail: books@gyanbooks.com

Distribution Network
gyanbooks.com
India, USA, Canada, UK, Australia, France

ISBN : 978-81-212-9442-3 (PB)
First Published, 1920

2nd Impression 2023

Printed at: Gyan Press, Delhi.

VEDANTA PHILOSOPHY RAJA YOGA
Author: SWAMI VIVEKANANDA

RÂJA YOGA

SWÂMI VIVEKÂNANDA

REPRESENTATIVE OF THE HINDU RELIGION AT THE WORLD'S PARLIAMENT OF RELIGIONS, HELD IN CHICAGO, 1893

VEDANTA PHILOSOPHY

RÂJA YOGA

BEING LECTURES BY THE

SWÂMI VIVEKÂNANDA

WITH PATANJALI'S APHORISMS, COMMENTARIES
AND A GLOSSARY OF TERMS

NEW EDITION, WITH ENLARGED GLOSSARY

NEW YORK
BRENTANO'S
1920

EACH SOUL IS POTENTIALLY DIVINE.

THE GOAL IS TO MANIFEST THIS DIVINITY WITHIN, BY CONTROLLING NATURE, EXTERNAL AND INTERNAL.

DO THIS EITHER BY WORK, OR WORSHIP, OR PSYCHIC CONTROL, OR PHILOSOPHY, BY ONE, OR MORE, OR ALL OF THESE— AND BE FREE.

THIS IS THE WHOLE OF RELIGION. DOCTRINES, OR DOGMAS, OR RITUALS, OR BOOKS, OR TEMPLES, OR FORMS, ARE BUT SECONDARY DETAILS.

PREFACE

SINCE the dawn of history, various extraordinary phenomena have been recorded as happening amongst human beings. Witnesses are not wanting in modern times to attest to the fact of such events, even in societies living under the full blaze of modern science. The vast mass of such evidence is unreliable, as coming from ignorant, superstitious, or fraudulent persons. In many instances the so-called miracles are imitations. But what do they imitate? It is not the sign of a candid and scientific mind to throw overboard anything without proper investigation. Surface scientists, unable to explain the various extraordinary mental phenomena, strive to ignore their very existence. They are, therefore, more culpable than those who think that their prayers are answered by a being, or beings, above the clouds, or than those who believe that their petitions will make such beings change the course of the universe. The latter have the excuse of ignorance, or at least of a false system of education in their childhood, which has taught them to depend upon such beings for help, and this dependence has now become a part of their degenerate nature. The former have no such excuse.

For thousands of years such phenomena have been investigated, studied, and generalised, the whole ground of the religious faculties of man has been analysed, and the practical result is the science of *Râja Yoga*. *Râja Yoga* does not, after the unpardonable manner of some modern scientists, deny the existence of facts which are very difficult to explain; on the other hand, it gently, yet in no uncertain terms, tells the superstitious that miracles and answers to prayers, and powers of faith, though true as facts, are not rendered comprehensible through the superstitious explanation of attributing them to the agency of a being, or beings, above the clouds. It declares to mankind that each being is only a conduit for the infinite ocean of knowledge and power that lies behind. It teaches that desires and wants are in man, that the power of supply is also in man; and that wherever and whenever a desire, a want, a prayer, has been fulfilled, it was out of this infinite magazine that the supply came, and not from any supernatural being. The idea of supernatural beings may rouse to a certain extent the power of action in man, but it also brings spiritual decay. It brings dependence; it brings fear; it brings superstition. It degenerates into a horrible belief in the natural weakness of man. There is no supernatural, says the *Yogî*, but there are in nature gross manifestations and subtle manifestations. The subtle are the causes, the gross the effects. The gross can be easily perceived by the senses; not so the subtle. The practice of *Râja Yoga* will lead to the acquisition of the more subtle perceptions.

All the orthodox systems of Indian philosophy have one goal in view, the liberation of the soul through perfection. The method is by *Yoga*. The word *Yoga* covers an immense ground, but both the *Sânkhya* and the *Vedântist* Schools point to *Yoga* in some form or other.

The subject of the first lectures in the present book is that form of *Yoga* known as *Râja Yoga*. The aphorisms of *Patanjali* are the highest authority and text book on *Râja Yoga*. The other philosophers, though occasionally differing from *Patanjali* in some philosophical aspect, have, as a rule, acceded to his method of practice a decided consent. The first part of this book is comprised of several lectures to classes delivered by the present writer in New York. The second part is a rather free translation of the aphorisms (*Sûtras*) of *Patanjali*, with a running commentary. Effort has been made to avoid technicalities as far as possible, and to keep to the free and easy style of conversation. In the first part some simple and specific directions are given for the student who wants to practise, but all such are especially and earnestly reminded that, with few exceptions, *Yoga* can only be safely learned by direct contact with a teacher. If these conversations succeed in awakening a desire for further information on the subject, the teacher will not be wanting.

The system of *Patanjali* is based upon the system of the *Sânkhyas*, the points of difference being very few.

The two most important differences are, first that *Patanjali* admits a Personal God in the form of a first teacher, while the only God the *Sânkhyas* admit is a nearly perfected being, temporarily in charge of a cycle. Second, the *Yogîs* hold the mind to be equally all-pervading with the soul, or *Puruṣa*, and the *Sânkhyas* do not.

THE AUTHOR.

CONTENTS

RÂJA YOGA.

PAGE.

Preface ix

Chap.

I. Introductory 1

II. The First Steps 17

III. Prâna 29

IV. The Psychic Prâna 47

V. The control of Psychic Prâna . . . 55

VI. Pratyâhâra and Dhâranâ 62

VII. Dhyâna and Samdâhi 72

VIII. Râja Yoga in brief 86

PATANJALI'S YOGA APHORISMS.

Introduction 97

I. Concentration: its Spiritual uses . . 104

II. " its Practice . . . 147

CHAP. PAGE.

III. THE CHAPTER OF POWERS 189

IV. INDEPENDENCE 207

APPENDIX 224

GLOSSARY 229

ओं
ओं तत् सत्

RÂJA YOGA

OR

CONQUERING THE INTERNAL NATURE

CHAPTER I.

INTRODUCTORY.

ALL our knowledge is based upon experience. What we call inferential knowledge, in which we go from the less general to the more general, or from the general to the particular, has experience as its basis. In what are called the exact sciences, people easily find the truth, because it appeals to the particular experiences of every human being. The scientist does not tell you to believe in anything, but he has certain results which come from his own experiences, and reasoning on these experiences, when he asks us to believe in his conclusions, he appeals to some universal experience of humanity. In every exact science there is a universal basis which is common to all humanity, so that we can at once see the truth or the fallacy of the conclusions drawn therefrom. Now, the question is, has religion any such basis or not? I shall have to answer the question both in the affirmative and in the negative. Religion, as it is generally taught all over the world, is said to be based upon faith and belief, and, in most cases, consists only of different sets of theories, and that is the reason why we find all these various religions quarrelling with each other. These theories, again, are based upon belief. One man says there is a great Being sitting above the clouds and governing the whole universe, and he asks me to believe that, solely on the authority of his assertion. In the same way I may have my own ideas, which I am asking others to believe, and if they ask a reason, I cannot supply them with any. This is why religion and metaphysical philosophy have a bad name nowadays. Every educated man seems to say: "Oh, these religions are only bundles of theories without any standard to judge them by, each man preaching his own pet ideas." At the same time I must tell you that there is a basis of universal belief in religion, governing all these different theories, and all the varying ideas of different sects of men in different countries. Going to the basis of them we find that they also are based upon universal experiences.

In the first place I will ask you to analyse all the various religions of the world. You will find that these are divided into two classes, those with a book, and those without a book. Those with a book are the strongest, and have the largest number of followers. Those without books have mostly died out, and the few new ones have very small followings. Yet, in all of them we find one consensus of opinion, that the truths they teach are the results of the experiences of particular persons.

The Christian asks you to believe in his religion, to believe in Christ, and to believe in Him as the incarnation of God, to believe in a God, in a soul, and in a better state of that soul. If I ask him for reasons he says, "No, it is my belief." But if you go to the fountain head of Christianity you will find that it is based upon experience. Christ said He saw God; the disciples said they felt God; and so forth. Similarly, in Buddhism, it is Buddha's experience — He experienced certain truths, saw them, came in contact with them, and preached them to the world. So with the Hindus — in their book the writers, who are called *Rishîs*, or sages, declare they have experienced certain truths, and these they preach. Thus it is clear that all the religions of the world have been built upon that one universal and adamantine foundation of all our knowledge — direct experience. The teachers all saw God; they all saw their own souls, they saw their eternity, they saw their future, and what they saw they preached. Only there is this difference, that in most of these religions, especially in modern times, a peculiar claim is put before us, and that claim is that these experiences are impossible at the present day; they were only possible with a few men, who were the first founders of the religions that subsequently bore their names. At the present time these experiences have become obsolete, and therefore we have now to take religion on belief. This I entirely deny. If there has been one case of experience in this world in any particular branch of knowledge it absolutely follows that this experience has been possible millions of times before, and will be repeated eternally. Uniformity is the rigorous law of nature; what once happened can happen always.

The teachers of the science of *Yoga*, therefore, declare that religion is not only based upon the experience of ancient times, but that no man can be religious until he has the same perceptions himself. *Yoga* is the science which teaches us how to get these perceptions. It is useless to talk about religion until one has felt it. Why is there so much disturbance, so much fighting and quarrelling in the name of God? There has been more bloodshed in the name of God than for any other cause, and the reason is that people never went to the fountain head; they were content only to give a mental assent to the customs of their forefathers, and wanted others to do the same. What right has a man to say he has a soul if he does not feel it, or that there is a God if he does not see Him? If there is a God we must see Him, if there is a soul we must perceive it; otherwise it is better not to believe. It is better to be an outspoken atheist than a hypocrite. The modern idea, on the one hand, with the "learned," is that religion and metaphysics, and all search after a Supreme Being, is futile; on the other hand, with the semi-educated, the idea seems to be that these things really have no basis, that their only value consists in the fact that they are strong motive powers for doing good to the world. If men believe in a God, they may become good, and moral, and so make good citizens. We cannot blame them for holding such ideas, seeing that all the teaching these men get is simply to believe in an eternal rigmarole of words, without any substance behind them. They are asked to live upon words; can they do it? If they could, I should not have the least regard for human nature. Man wants truth, wants to experience truth for himself, to grasp it, to realise it, to feel it within his heart of hearts; then alone, declare the *Vedas*, will all doubts vanish, all darkness be scattered, and all crookedness be made straight. "Ye children of immortality, even those who live in the highest sphere, the way is found; there is a way out of all this darkness, and that is by perceiving Him Who is beyond all darkness, and there is no other way."

The science of *Râja Yoga* proposes to put before humanity a practical and scientifically worked-out method of reaching this truth. In the first place, every science must have its own method of investigation. If you want to become an astronomer, and sit down and cry "Astronomy, astronomy!" it will never come to you. The same with chemistry. A certain method must be followed. You must go to the laboratory, take the different substances, mix them up, compound them, experiment with them, and out of that will come a knowledge of chemistry. If you want to be an astronomer you must go to the observatory, take a telescope, study the stars and planets, and then you will become an astronomer. Each science must have its own methods. I could preach you thousands of sermons, but they would not make you religious, until you first practised the method. These are the truths of the sages of all countries, of all ages, men pure and unselfish, who had no motive but to do good to the world. They all declare that they have found some truth higher than that the senses can bring to us, and they challenge verification. They say to you, take up the method and practise honestly, and then, if you do not find this higher truth, you will have the right to say there is no truth in the claim, but before you have done that, you are not rational in denying the truth of these assertions. So we must work faithfully, using the prescribed methods, and light will come.

In acquiring knowledge we make use of generalisation, and generalisation is based upon observation. We first observe facts, and then we generalise, and then we draw our conclusions or principles. The knowledge of the mind, of the internal nature of man, of thought, can never be had until we have the power of first observing the facts that are going on within. It is very easy to observe facts in the external world, and many thousand instruments have been invented to observe every point of nature, but in the internal world we find no instrument to help us. Yet we know we must observe in order to have a real science. Without a proper analysis, any science will be hopeless, mere theorising, and that is why all the psychologists have been quarrelling among themselves since the beginning of time, except those few who found out the means of observation.

The science of *Râja Yoga*, in the first place, proposes to give men such a means of observing the internal states, and the instrument is the mind itself. The power of attention of mind, when properly guided, and directed towards the internal world, will analyse the mind, and illumine facts for us.' The powers of the mind are like rays of light being dissipated; when they are concentrated they illumine everything. This is the only source of knowledge that we have. Everyone is using it, both in the external and the internal world, but, for the psychologist, this minute observation which the scientific man can throw upon the external world, will have to be thrown on the internal world, and this requires a great deal of practice. From our childhood upwards we have been taught only to pay attention to things external, never to pay attention to things internal, and most of us have nearly lost the faculty of observing the internal mechanism. To turn the mind, as it were, inside, stop it from going outside, and then to concentrate all its powers, and throw them upon the mind itself, in order that it may know its own nature, analyse itself, is very hard work. Yet that is the only way to anything which will be a scientific approach to the subject.

What is the use of such knowledge? In the first place, knowledge itself is the highest reward of knowledge, and, in the second place, there is also utility in it. It will take away all our misery. When, by analysing his own mind, man comes face to face, as it were, with something which is never destroyed, something which is, by its own nature, eternally pure and perfect, he will no more be miserable, no more unhappy. All misery comes from fear, from unsatisfied desire. Man will find that he never dies, and then he will have no more fear of death. When he knows that he is perfect, he will have no more vain desires, and both these causes being absent, there will be no more misery — there will be perfect bliss, even while in this body.

There is only one method by which to attain this knowledge, that which is called concentration. The chemist in his laboratory concentrates all the energies of his mind into one focus, and throws them out upon the materials he is analysing, and so finds out their secret. The astronomer concentrates all the energies of his mind and projects them through his telescope upon the skies; and the stars, the sun, and the moon, give up their secrets to him. The more I can concentrate my thoughts on the matter on which I am talking to you, the more light I can throw upon it. You are listening to me, and the more you concentrate your thoughts the more clearly you will grasp what I have to say.

How has all this knowledge in the world been gained but by the concentration of the powers of the mind? Nature is ready to give up her secrets if we only know how to knock, to give her the necessary blow, and the strength and force of the blow come through concentration. There is no limit to the power of the human mind. The more concentrated it is, the more power is brought to bear on one point, and that is the secret.

It is easier to concentrate the mind on external things, the mind naturally goes outwards; but, in the case of religion, or psychology, or metaphysics, the subject and object are one. The object is internal, the mind itself is the object, and it is necessary to study the mind itself, mind studying mind. We know that there is the power of the mind called reflective. I am talking to you; at the same time I am standing aside, as it were, a second person, and knowing and hearing what I am talking. You work and think at the same time, another portion of your mind stands by and sees what you are thinking. The powers of the mind should be concentrated and turned back upon itself, and as the darkest places reveal their secrets before the penetrating rays of the sun, so will this concentrated mind penetrate its own innermost secrets. Thus will we come to the basis of belief, the real genuine religion. We will perceive for ourselves whether we have souls, whether life is of five minutes, or of eternity, whether there is a God in the universe or none. It will all be revealed to us. This is what *Râja Yoga* proposes to teach. The goal of all its teaching is how to concentrate the mind, then how to discover the facts in our own minds, then how to generalise those facts, and form our own conclusions from them. It therefore never asks the question what our religion is, whether we are Deists, or Atheists, whether Christians, Jews, or Buddhists. We are human beings; that is sufficient. Every human being has the right and the power to seek for religion; every human being has the right to ask the reason why, and to have his question answered by himself, if he only takes the trouble.

So far, then, we see that in the study of this *Râja Yoga* no faith or belief is necessary. Believe nothing until you find it out for yourself; that is what it teaches us. Truth requires no prop to make it stand. Do you mean to say that the facts of our awakened state require any dreams or imaginings to prove them? Certainly not. This study of *Râja Yoga* takes a long time and constant practice. A part of this practice is physical, but the main part of it is mental. As we go along we shall find how intimately the mind is connected with the body. If we believe that the mind is simply a finer part of the body, and that mind acts upon the body, in the same way the body must act upon the mind. If the body is sick, the mind becomes sick also. If the body is healthy, the mind remains healthy and strong. When one is angry, the mind becomes disturbed; at the same time, when the mind is disturbed, the body also becomes disturbed. With the majority of mankind the mind is entirely under the control of the body; the mind is very little developed. The vast mass of humanity, if you will kindly excuse me, is very little removed from the animals. Not only that, but, in many instances, the power of control is very little higher than that of the lower animals. We have very little command of our minds. Therefore to bring that command about, to get that control over body and mind, we must take certain physical helps, and when the body is sufficiently controlled, we can attempt the manipulation of the mind. By manipulation of the mind, we shall be able to bring it under our control, make it work as we like, and compel it to concentrate its powers as we desire.

According to the *Râja Yogî*, all this external world is but the gross form of the internal, or subtle. The finer is always the cause, and the grosser the effect. So the external world is the effect, and the internal the cause. In the same way external forces are simply the grosser parts, of which the internal forces are the finer. One who has discovered and learned how to manipulate the internal forces will get the whole of nature under his control. The *Yogî* proposes to himself no less a task than to master the whole universe, to control the whole of nature. He wants to arrive at the point where what we call "nature's laws" will have no influence over him, where he will be able to get beyond them all. He will be master of the whole of nature, internal and external. The progress and civilisation of the human race is simply controlling this nature.

Various races differ in their processes. Just as in the same society some individuals want to control external nature, and others want to control internal nature, so, among races, some want to control the external nature, and some the internal. Some say that by controlling internal nature we control everything; some that by controlling external nature we control everything. Carried to the extreme both are right, because there is neither internal nor external. It is a fictitious limitation that never existed. Both are destined to meet at the same point, the externalists and the internalists, when both reach the extreme of their knowledge. Just as the physician, when he pushes his knowledge to its limits, finds it melting away into metaphysics, so the metaphysician will find that what he calls mind and matter are but apparent distinctions, which will have to vanish for ever.

The end and aim of all science is to find a unit, that One out of which all this manifold is being manufactured, that One existing as many. *Râja Yoga* proposes to start from the internal world, to study internal nature, and, through that, control the whole — both internal and external. It is a very old attempt. India has been its special stronghold but it was also attempted by other nations. In Western countries it is thought to be mysticism. People who wanted to practise it were either burned or killed as witches and sorcerers, and in India, for various reasons, it fell into the hands of persons who destroyed 90 per cent. of the knowledge, and of that portion which remained tried to make a great secret. In modern times many so-called teachers have arisen worse than those of India, because the latter knew something, while these modern exponents do not.

Anything that is secret and mysterious in these systems of *Yoga* should be at once rejected. The best guide in life is strength. In religion, as in everything else, discard everything that weakens you, have nothing to do with it. All mystery-mongering weakens the human brain. Through it this science of *Yoga* has been well nigh destroyed, but it is really one of the grandest of sciences. From the time that it was discovered, more than 4000 years ago, it was perfectly delineated and formulated and preached in India, and it is a striking fact, that the more modern the commentator, the greater the mistakes he makes. The more ancient the writer on it the more rational he is. Most of the modern writers talk of all sorts of mystery. Thus it fell into the hands of a few persons who made it a secret, instead of letting the full blaze of daylight and reason fall upon it, and they did so that they might have the powers to themselves.

In the first place there is no mystery in what I preach. What little I know I will tell you. So far as I can reason it out I will do so, but what I do not know I will simply tell you that it is what the books say. It is wrong to blindly believe. You must exercise your own reason and judgment; you must practise, and see whether these things happen or not. Just as you would take up any other science of a material nature, exactly in the same manner you should take up this science for study. There is neither mystery nor danger in it. So far as it is true it ought to be preached in the public streets, in the broad daylight. Any attempt to mystify these things is productive of great danger.

Before proceeding further, I will state to you a little of the *Sânkhya* Philosophy, upon which the whole of *Râja Yoga* is based. According to this philosophy perception comes through instruments, *e. g.*, the eyes; the eyes carry it to the organs, the organs to the mind, the mind to the determinative faculty, from this the *Puruṣa* (the soul) receives it, and gives the order back, as it were, and so on through all these stages. In this way sensations are received. With the exception of the

Puruṣa all of these are material, but the mind is of much finer material than the external instruments. That material of which the mind is composed becomes grosser, and becomes what is called the *Tanmâtras* It becomes still grosser and forms the external material. That is the psychology of the *Sânkhya*. So that, between the intellect and the grosser matter outside there is only a difference in degree. The *Puruṣa* is the only thing which is immaterial. Mind is an instrument in the hands of the soul, as it were, through which the soul catches external objects. This mind is constantly changing and vacillating, and it can either attach itself to several organs, or to one, or to none. For instance, if I hear the clock with great attention I will not, perhaps, see anything, although my eyes may be open, showing that the mind was not attached to the seeing organ, although it was to the hearing organ. And the mind, in the same way, can be attached to all the organs simultaneously. This mind has the reflexive power of looking back into its own depths. This reflexive power is what the *Yogî* wants to attain; by concentrating the powers of the mind, and turning them inward, he seeks to know what is happening inside. There is in this no question of mere belief; it is the analysis of certain philosophers. Modern physiologists tell you that the eyes are not the organs of vision, but that the organs are in the nerve centre in the brain, and so with all the senses; and they also tell you that these centres are formed of the same material as the brain itself. So the *Sânkhyas* will also tell you, but one is a statement on the physical side, and the other on the psychological side; yet both are the same. Beyond this we have to demonstrate.

The *Yogî* proposes to himself to attain to that fine state of perception in which he can perceive all these things. There must be mental perception of all the different states. We shall perceive how the sensation is travelling, and how the mind is receiving it, how it is going to the determinative faculty, and how this gives it to the *Puruṣa*. As each science requires certain preparations, as each science has its own method, until we follow that method we can never understand that science; so in *Râja Yoga*.

Certain regulations as to food are necessary; we must use that food which brings us the purest mind. If you go into a menagerie you will find this demonstrated at once. You see the elephants, huge animals, but calm and gentle; and if you go toward the cages of the lions and tigers you will find them restless, showing how much difference has been produced by food. All the forces that are working in this body have been produced out of food; we see that every day. If you begin to fast, first your body will get weak, the physical forces will suffer; then, after a few days, the mental forces will suffer also. First, memory will fail. Then comes a point, when you are not able to think, much less to pursue any course of reasoning. We have, therefore, to take care what sort of food we eat at the beginning, and when we have got strength enough, when our practice is well advanced, we need not be so careful in this respect. While the plant is growing it must be hedged round, lest it be injured; but when it becomes a tree the hedges are taken away; it is strong enough to withstand all assaults.

A *Yogî* must avoid the two extremes of luxury and austerity. He must not fast, or torture his flesh; he who does so, says the *Gîtâ*, cannot be a *Yogî;* he who fasts; he who keeps awake; he who sleeps much; he who works too much; he who does no work; none of these can be *Yogîs*.

CHAPTER II.

THE FIRST STEPS.

RÂJA YOGA is divided into eight steps. The first is *Yama* — non-killing, truthfulness, non-stealing, continence, and non-receiving of any gifts. Next is *Niyama* — cleanliness, contentment, mortification, study, and self-surrender to God. Then comes *Âsana*, or posture; *Prâṇâyâma*, or controlling the vital forces of the body; *Pratyâhâra*, or making the mind introspective; *Dhâranâ*, or concentration; *Dhyânâ*, or meditation; and *Samâdhi*, or super-consciousness. The *Yama* and *Niyama*, as we see, are moral trainings; without these as the basis no practice of *Yoga* will succeed. As these practices become established the *Yogî* will begin to realise the fruits of his practice; without these it will never bear fruit. A *Yogî* must not think of injuring anyone, through thought, word or deed, and this applies not only to man, but to all animals. Mercy shall not be for men alone, but shall go beyond, and embrace the whole world.

The next step is *Âsana*, posture; a series of exercises, physical and mental, is to be gone through every day, until certain higher states are reached. Therefore it is quite necessary that we should find a posture in which we can remain long. That posture which is easiest for each one is the posture to use. For one man it may be very easy to think in a certain posture, but this may be very difficult for another. We will find later on that in the study of these psychological matters there will be a good deal of action going on in the body. Nerve currents will have to be displaced and given a new channel. New sorts of vibrations will begin, the whole constitution will be remodelled, as it were. But the main part of the action will lie along the spinal column, so that the one thing necessary for the posture is to hold the spinal column free, sitting erect, holding the three parts — the chest, neck, and head — in a straight line. Let the whole weight of the body be supported by the ribs, and then you have an easy natural posture, with the spine straight. You will naturally see that you cannot think very high thoughts with the chest in. This portion of the *Yoga* is a little similar to the *Hatha Yoga*, which deals entirely with the physical body; the aim of the latter is to make the physical body very strong. We have notning to do with that here, because its practices are very difficult, and cannot be learned in a day, and, after all, do not lead to any spiritual growth. Many of these practices you will find in Delsarte, and other teachers, such as placing the body in different postures, but the object in these is physical, not psychological. There is not one muscle in the body over which a man cannot establish a perfect control; the heart can be made to stop or go on at his bidding, and, in the same way, each part of the organism can be made to work at his bidding.

The result of this part of *Yoga* is to make men live long; health is the chief idea, the one goal of the *Hatha Yogî*. He is determined not to fall sick, and he never does. He lives long; a hundred years is nothing to him; he is quite young and fresh when he is 150, without one hair turned grey. But that is all. A *Banyan* tree lives sometimes 5000 years, but it is a *Banyan* tree and nothing more. So, if a man lives long, he is only a healthy animal. One or two ordinary lessons of the *Hatha Yogîs* are very useful. For instance, some of you will find it a good thing for headaches to drink cold water through the nose as soon as you get up; the whole day your brain will be nice and cool, and you will never catch cold. It is very easy to do; put your nose into the water, and make a pump action in the throat.

After one has learned to have a firm erect seat, he has to perform, according to certain schools, a practice called the purifying of the nerves. This part has been rejected by some as not belonging to *Râja Yoga*, but as so great an authority as the commentator, *Śankarâchârya*, advises it, I think it fit that it should be mentioned, and I will quote his own directions from his commentary to the *Svetâśvatara Upaniṣad*. "The mind whose dross has been cleared away by *Prâṇâyâma*, becomes fixed in *Brahman;* therefore *Prâṇâyâma* is pointed out. First the nerves are to be purified, then comes the power to practise *Prâṇâyâma*. Stopping the right nostril with the thumb, with the left nostril fill in air, according to one's capacity; then, without any interval, throw the air out through the right nostril, closing the left one. Again inhaling through the right nostril eject through the left, according to capacity; practising this three or five times at four intervals of the day, before dawn, during midday, in the evening, and at midnight, in fifteen days or a month purity of the nerves is attained; then begins *Prâṇâyâma.*"

Practice is absolutely necessary. You may sit down and listen to me by the hour every day, but, if you do not practise, you will not get one step further. It all depends on practice. We never understand these things until we experience them. We will have to see and feel them for ourselves. Simply listening to explanations and theories will not do. There are several obstructions to practice. The first obstruction is an unhealthy body; if the body is not in a fit state, the practice will be obstructed. Therefore we have to keep the body in good health; we have to take care of what we eat and drink, and what we do; always use a mental effort, what is usually called "Christian Science," to keep the body strong. That is all; nothing further of the body. We must not forget that health is only a means to an end. If health were the end we would be like animals; animals rarely become unhealthy.

The second obstruction is doubt; we always feel doubtful about things we do not see. Man cannot live upon words, however he may try. So, doubt comes to us as to whether there is any truth in these things or not; even the best of us will doubt sometimes. With practice, within a few days, a little glimpse will come, enough to give you encouragement and hope. As one commentator on *Yoga* philosophy says: "When one proof is realised, however little it may be, that will give us faith in the whole teachings of *Yoga*." For instance, after the first few months of training and teaching, you will begin to find you can read another's thoughts; they will come to you in picture form. Perhaps you will hear something happening at a long distance, when you concentrate your mind and try to do so. These glimpses will come, just a little bit at first, but enough to give you faith, and strength, and hope. For instance, if you concentrate your thoughts on the tip of your nose, in a few days you will begin to smell most beautiful fragrance, and that will be enough to show you that there are certain mental perceptions that can be made obvious without the contact of physical objects. But we must always remember that these are only the means; the aim, and end, and goal, of all this training is liberation of the soul. Absolute control of nature, and nothing short of it, must be the goal. We must be the masters, and not nature; neither body nor mind must be our master, and neither must we forget that the body is mine, and not I the body's.

A god and a demon went to learn about the Self from a great sage. They studied with him for a long time, and at last the sage told them, "Thou thyself art the being thou art seeking." Both of them thought that their bodies were the Self. "We have got everything," they said, and both of them returned to their people and said, "We have learned everything that is to be learned; eat, drink, and be merry; we are the Self; there is nothing beyond us." The nature of the demon was ignorant, clouded, so he never inquired any further, but was perfectly satisfied with the idea that he was God, that by the Self was meant the body. But the god had a purer nature. He at first committed the mistake of thinking, "I, this body, am *Brahman*, so keep it strong and in health, and well-dressed, and give it all sorts of bodily enjoyments." But, in a few days, he found out that this could not be the meaning of the sage, their master; there must be something higher. So he came back and said, "Sir, did you teach me that this body is the Self? If so, I see all bodies die; the Self cannot die." The sage said, "Find it out; thou art That." Then the god thought that the vital forces which work the body were what the sage meant. But, after a time, he found that if he ate, these vital forces remained strong, but, if he starved, they became weak. The god then went back to the sage and said, "Sir, do you mean that the vital forces are the Self?" The sage said, "Find out for yourself; thou art That." The god returned once more, and thought that it was the mind; perhaps that is the Self. But in a few days he reflected that thoughts are so various; now good, now bad; the mind is too changeable to be the Self. He went back to the sage and said, "Sir, I do not think that the mind is the

Self; did you mean that?" "No," replied the sage, "thou art That; find out for yourself." The god went back, and, at last, found that he was the Self, beyond all thought; One, without birth or death, whom the sword cannot pierce, or the fire burn, whom the air cannot dry, or the water melt, the beginningless and birthless, the immovable, the intangible, the omniscient, the omnipotent Being, and that it was neither the body nor the mind, but beyond them all. So he was satisfied, but the poor demon did not get the truth, owing to his fondness for the body.

This world has a good many of these demoniac natures, but there are some gods too. If one propose to teach any science to increase the power of sense enjoyment, he finds multitudes ready for it. If one undertake to show mankind the supreme goal, they care nothing for that. Very few have the power to grasp the highest, fewer still the patience to attain to it, but a few also know that if the body be kept for a thousand years the result will be the same in the end. When the forces that hold it together go away the body must fall. No man was ever born who could stop his body one moment from changing. Body is the name of a series of changes. "As in a river the masses of water are changing before you every moment, and new masses are coming, yet taking similar form, so is it with this body." Yet the body must be kept strong and healthy; it is the best instrument we have.

This human body is the greatest body in the universe, and a human being the greatest being. Man is higher than all animals, than all angels; none is greater than man. Even the *Devas* will have to come down again and attain to salvation through a human body. Man alone attains to perfection, not even the devas. According to the Jews and Mohammedans God created man after creating the angels and everything else, and after creating man He asked the angels to come and salute him, and all did except Iblis; so God cursed him and he became Satan. Behind this allegory is the great truth, that this human birth is the greatest birth we can have. The lower creation, the animal, is dull, and manufactured mostly out of *Tamas*. Animals cannot have any high thoughts; nor can the angels, or Devas, attain to direct freedom without human birth. In human society, in the same way, too much wealth, or too much poverty, is a great impediment to the higher development of the soul. It is from the middle classes that the great ones of the world come. Here the forces are very equally adjusted and balanced.

Returning to our subject, we come next to *Prâṇâyâma*, controlling the breathing. What has that to do with concentrating the powers of the mind? Breath is like the fly-wheel of this machine. In a big engine you find the fly-wheel first moving, and that motion is conveyed to finer and finer machinery, until the most delicate and finest mechanism in the machine is in motion in accordance. This breath is that fly-wheel, supplying and regulating the motive power to everything in this body.

There was once a minister to a great king. He fell into disgrace, and the king as a punishment, ordered him to be shut up in the top of a very high tower. This was done, and the minister was left there to perish. He had a faithful wife, however, and at night she came to the tower and called to her husband at the top to know what she could do to help him. He told her to return to the tower the following night and bring with her a long rope, a stout twine, a pack thread, a silken thread, a beetle, and a little honey. Wondering much, the good wife obeyed her husband, and brought him the desired articles. The husband directed her to attach the silken thread firmly to the beetle, then to smear his horns with a drop of honey, and to set him free on the wall of the tower, with his head pointing upwards. She obeyed all these instructions, and the beetle started on his long journey. Smelling the honey before him he slowly crept onwards and onwards, in the hope of reaching it, until at last he reached the top of the tower, when the minister grasped the beetle, and got possession of the silken thread. He told his wife to tie the other end to the pack thread, and after he had drawn up the pack thread, he repeated the process with the stout twine, and lastly with the rope. Then the rest was easy. The minister descended from the tower by means of the rope, and made his escape. In this body of ours the breath motion is the "silken thread," and laying hold of that, and learning to control it we grasp the pack thread of the nerve currents, and from these the stout twine of our thoughts, and lastly the rope of *Prâṇa*, controlling which we reach freedom.

We do not know anything about our own bodies;

we cannot know. At best we can take a dead body, and cut it in pieces, and there are some who can take a live animal and cut it in pieces in order to see what is inside the body. Still, that has nothing to do with our own bodies. We know very little about them; why do we not? Because our attention is not discriminating enough to catch the very fine movements that are going on within. We can know of them only as the mind, as it were, enters the body, and becomes more subtle. To get that subtle perception we have to begin with the grosser perceptions, so we have to get hold of that which is setting the whole engine in motion, and that is the *Prâṇa*, the most obvious manifestation of which is the breath. Then, along with the breath, we will slowly enter the body, and that will enable us to find out about the subtle forces, how the nerve currents are moving all over the body, and as soon as we perceive that, and learn to feel them, we shall begin to get control over them, and over the body. The mind is also set in motion by these different nerve currents, so, at last, we shall reach the state when we have perfect control over the body and mind, making both our servants. Knowledge is power, and we have to get this power, so we must begin at the beginning, the *Prâṇâyâmâ* restraining the *Prâṇa*. This *Prâṇâyâma* is a long subject, and will take several lessons to illustrate it thoroughly. We will take it part by part.

We shall gradually see what are the reasons for each exercise and what forces in the body are set in motion. All these things will come to us, but it requires constant practice, and the proof will come by practice. No amount of reasoning which I can give you will be proof to you, until you have demostrated it for your-selves. As soon as you begin to feel these currents in motion all over you, doubts will vanish, but it requires hard practice every day. You must practise at least twice every day, and the best times are towards the morning and the evening. When night passes into day, and day into night, it has to pass through a state of relative calmness. The early morning and the early evening are the two points of calmness. Your body will have a like tendency to become calm at those times. We will take advantage of that natural condition, and begin then to practise. Make it a rule not to eat until you have practised; if you do this the sheer force of hunger will break your laziness. In India they teach children never to eat until they have practised, and worshipped, and it becomes natural to them after a time; a boy will not feel hungry until he has bathed and practised.

Those of you who can afford it will do better to have a room for this practice alone; do not sleep in that room, it must be kept holy; you must not enter the room until you have bathed, and are perfectly clean in body and mind. Place flowers in that room always; they are the best surroundings for a *Yogî;* also pictures that are pleasing. Burn incense morning and evening. Have no quarrelling, or anger, or unholy thought in that room. Only allow those persons to enter who are of the same thought as you. Then by and by there will be an atmosphere of holiness in the room, and when you are miserable, sorrowful, doubtful, or your mind is disturbed, the very fact of entering that room will make you calmer. This was the idea of the temple and the church, and in some temples and churches you will find it even now, but in the majority of them the very idea has been lost. The idea is that by keeping holy vibrations there the place becomes and remains illumined. Those who cannot afford to have a room set apart can practise anywhere they like. Sit in a straight posture, and the first thing to do is to send a current of holy thought to all creation; mentally repeat: "Let all beings be happy; let all beings be peaceful; let all beings be blissful." So do to the East, South, North and West. The more you do that the better you will feel yourself. You will find at last that the easiest way to make yourselves healthy is to see that others are healthy, and the easiest way to make yourselves happy is to see that others are happy. After doing that, those who believe in God should pray — not for money, not for health, nor for heaven; pray for knowledge and light; every other prayer is selfish. Then the next thing to do is to think of your own body, and see that it is strong and healthy; it is the best instrument you have. Think of it as being as strong as adamant, and that with the help of this body you will cross this ocean of life. Freedom is never to be reached by the weak; throw away all weakness; tell your body that it is strong; tell your mind that it is strong, and have unbounded faith and hope in yourself.

CHAPTER III.

PRÂṆA.

PRÂṆÂYÂMA is not, as many think, something about the breath; breath, indeed, has very little to do with it, if anything. Breathing is only one of the many exercises through which we get to the real *Prâṇâyâma*. *Prâṇâyâma* means the control of *Prâṇa*. According to the philosophers of India, the whole universe is composed of two materials, one of which they call *Âkâśa*. It is the omnipresent, all penetrating existence. Everything that has form, everything that is the result of compounds, is evolved out of this *Âkâśa*. It is the *Âkâśa* that becomes the air, that becomes the liquids, that becomes the solids; it is the *Âkâśa* that becomes the sun, the earth, the moon, the stars, the comets; it is the *Âkâśa* that becomes the body, the animal body, the plants, every form that we see, everything that can be sensed, everything that exists. It itself cannot be perceived; it is so subtle that it is beyond all ordinary perception; it can only be seen when it has become gross, has taken form. At the beginning of creation there is only this *Âkâśa;* at the end of the cycle the solids, the liquids, and the gases all melt into the *Âkâśa* again, and the next creation similarly proceeds out of this *Âkâśa*.

By what power is this *Âkâśa* manufactured into this universe? By the power of *Prâṇa*. Just as *Âkâśa* is the infinite omnipresent material of this universe, so is this *Prâṇa* the infinite, omnipresent manifesting power of this universe. At the beginning and at the end of a cycle everything becomes *Âkâśa*, and all the forces that are in the universe resolve back into the *Prâṇa;* in the next cycle, out of this *Prâṇa* is evolved everything that we call energy, everything that we call force. It is the *Prâṇa* that is manifesting as motion; it is the *Prâṇa* that is manifesting as gravitation, as magnetism. It is the *Prâṇa* that is manifesting as the actions of the body, as the nerve currents, as thought force. From thought, down to the lowest physical force, everything is but the manifestation of *Prâṇa*. The sum-total of all force in the universe, mental or physical, when resolved back to its original state, is called *Prâṇa*. "When there was neither aught nor naught, when darkness was covering darkness, what existed then? That *Âkâśa* existed without motion." The physical motion of the *Prâṇa* was stopped, but it existed all the same. All the energies that are now displayed in the universe we know, by modern science, are unchangeable. The sum-total of the energies in the universe remains the same throughout, only, at the end of a cycle, these energies quiet down, become potential, and, at the beginning of the next cycle, they start up, strike upon the *Âkâśa*, and out of the *Âkâśa* evolve these various forms, and, as the *Âkâśa* changes, this *Prâṇa* changes also into all these manifestations of energy. The knowledge and control of this *Prâṇa* is really what is meant by *Prâṇâyâma*.

This opens to us the door to almost unlimited power. Suppose, for instance, one understood the *Prâṇa* perfectly, and could control it, what power on earth could there be that would not be his? He would be able to move the sun and stars out of their places, to control everything in the universe, from the atoms to the biggest suns, because he would control the *Prâṇa*. This is the end and aim of *Prâṇâyâma*. When the *Yogî* becomes perfect there will be nothing in nature not under his control. If he orders the gods to come, they will come at his bidding; if he asks the departed to come, they will come at his bidding. All the forces of nature will obey him as his slaves, and when the ignorant see these powers of the *Yogî* they call them miracles. One peculiarity of the Hindû mind is that it always inquires for the last possible generalisation, leaving the details to be worked out afterwards. The question is raised in the *Vedas*, "What is that, knowing which we shall know everything?" Thus, all books, and all philosophies that have been written, have been only to prove *That* by knowing which everything is known. If a man wants to know this universe bit by bit he must know every individual grain of sand, and that means infinite time for him; he cannot know all of them. Then how can knowledge be? How is it possible for a man to be all-knowing through particulars? The *Yogîs* say that behind this particular manifestation there is a generalisation. Behind all particular ideas stands a generalised, an abstract principle; grasp it, and you have grasped everything. Just as this whole universe has been generalised, in the *Vedas*, into that One Absolute Existence. He who has grasped that Existence has grasped the whole universe. So all forces have been generalised into this *Prâṇa*, and he who has grasped the *Prâṇa* has grasped all the forces of the universe, mental or physical. He who has controlled the *Prâṇa* has controlled his own mind, and all the minds that exist. He who has controlled the *Prâṇa* has controlled his body, and all the bodies that exist, because the *Prâṇa* is the generalised manifestation of force.

How to control the *Prâṇa* is the one idea of *Prâṇâyâma*. All these trainings and exercises are for that one end, and each man must begin where he stands, must learn how to control the things that are nearest to him. This body is the nearest thing to us, nearer than anything in the universe, and this mind is the nearest of all. The *Prâṇa* which is working this mind and body is the nearest to us of all the *Prâṇa* in the universe. This little wave of the *Prâṇa* which represents our own energies, mental and physical, is the nearest wave to us of all that infinite ocean of *Prâṇa*, and if we can succeed in controlling that little wave, then alone we can hope to control the whole of *Prâṇa*. Perfection is to be gained by the *Yogî* who has done this, and no power is any more his master. He has become almost almighty, almost all-knowing. We see sects in every country who have attempted this control of *Prâṇa*. In this country there are Mind-healers, Faith-healers, Spiritualists, Christian Scientists, Hypnotists, etc., and if we analyse these different groups we shall find that the background of each is this control of the *Prâṇa*, whether they know it or not. If you boil all their theories down the residuum will be the same. It is the one and same force they are manipulating, only unknowingly. They have stumbled on the discovery of a force, and do not know its nature, but they are unconsciously using the same powers which the *Yogî* uses, and which come from *Prâṇa*.

This *Prâṇa* is the vital force in every being, and the finest and highest action of *Prâṇa* is thought. This thought, again, as we see, is not all. There is also a sort of thought which we call instinct, or unconscious thought, the lowest plane of action. If a mosquito stings us, without thinking, our hand will strike it, automatically, instinctively. This is one expression of thought. All reflex actions of the body belong to this plane of thought. There is then a still higher plane of thought, the conscious. I reason, I judge, I think, I see the *pros* and *cons* of certain things; yet that is not all. We know that reason is limited. There is only a certain extent to which reason can go; beyond that it cannot reach. The circle within which it runs is very, very limited indeed. Yet, at the same time, we find facts rush into this circle. Like the coming of comets certain things are coming into this circle, and it is certain they come from outside the limit, although our reason cannot go beyond. The causes of the phenomena protruding themselves in this small limit are outside of this limit. The reason and the intellect cannot reach them, but, says the *Yogî*, that is not all. The mind can exist on a still higher plane, the super-conscious. When the mind has attained to that state, which is called *Samâdhi*,—perfect concentration, super-consciousness—it goes beyond the limits of reason, and comes face to face with facts which no instinct or reason can ever know. All these manipulations of the subtle forces of the body, the different manifestations of *Prâṇa*, if trained, give a push to the mind, and the mind goes up higher, and becomes super-conscious, and from that plane it acts.

In this universe there is one continuous mass on every plane of existence. Physically this universe is one; there is no difference between the sun and you. The scientist will tell you it is only a fiction to say the contrary. There is no real difference between the table and me; the table is one point in the mass of matter, and I another point. Each form represents, as it were, one whirlpool in the infinite ocean of matter, and these are not constant. Just as in a rushing stream there may be millions of whirlpools, and the water in each of these whirlpools is fresh every moment, turning round and round for a few seconds, and then passing out at the other end, and fresh particles of water coming in, so this whole universe is one constantly changing mass of matter, in which we are little whirlpools. A mass of matter enters them, goes round and round, and turns, for a few years, into the body of a man, becomes changed, and gets whirled out in the form of, maybe, an animal, from that it rushes round to get, after a few years, into another whirlpool, called a lump of mineral. It is a constant change. Not one body is constant. There is no such thing as my body, or your body, except in words. It is one huge mass of matter. One point is called moon, another sun, another a man, another the earth, another a plant, another a mineral. Not one is constant, but everything is changing, matter eternally concreting and disintregating. So it is with the mind. Matter is represented by the ether; when the action of *Prâṇa* is most subtle, this very ether, in the finer state of vibration, will represent the mind, and there it will be still one unbroken mass. If you can get to simply that subtle vibration you will see and feel that the whole universe is composed of these subtle vibrations. Sometimes certain drugs have the power to take us, as it were, through our senses, and bring us to that condition. Many of you may remember the celebrated experiment of Sir Humphrey Davy, when the laughing gas overpowered him, and, during the lecture, he remained motionless, stupefied, and, after that, he said that the whole universe was made up of ideas; for the time being, as it were, the gross vibrations had ceased, and only the subtle vibrations, which he called the mind, were present to him. He could only see the subtle vibrations round him; everything had become thought; the whole universe was an ocean of thought, he and everyone else had become little thought whirlpools.

Thus, even in the universe of thought we find this unity, and at last, when we get to the Self, we know that that Self can only be One. Beyond motion there is but One. Even in manifest motion there is only a unity. These facts can no more be denied, as modern science has demonstrated them. Modern physics also has demonstrated that the sum-total of the energies in the universe is the same throughout. It has also been proved that this sum-total of energy exists in two forms. It becomes potential, toned down, and calmed, and next it comes out manifested as all these various forces; again it goes back to the quiet state, and again it manifests. Thus it goes on evolving and involving through eternity. The control of this *Prâṇa*, as before stated, is what is called *Prâṇâyâma.*

This *Prâṇâyâma* has very little to do with breathing, except as exercise. The most obvious manifestation of this *Prâṇa* in the human body is the motion of the lungs. If that stops, the body will stop; all the other manifestations of force in the body will immediately stop, if this is stopped. There are persons who can train themselves in such a manner that the body will live on, even when this motion has stopped. There are some persons who can bury themselves for months and yet live, without breathing. But, for all ordinary persons, this is the principal gross motion in the body. To reach the more subtle we must take the help of the grosser, and so, slowly travel towards the most subtle, until we gain our point. The most obvious of all motions in the body is the motion of the lungs, the fly-wheel which is setting the other forces in motion. *Prâṇâyâma* really means controlling this motion of the lungs, and this motion is associated with the breath. Not that breath is producing it; on the contrary *it* is producing breath. This motion draws in the air by pump action. The *Prâṇa* is moving the lungs, and that motion of the lungs, draws in the air. So *Prâṇâyâma* is not breathing, but controlling that muscular power which moves the lungs, and that muscular power which is going out through the nerves to the muscles, from them to the lungs, making them move in a certain manner, is the *Prâṇa*, which we have to control in the practice of *Prâṇâyâma*. When this *Prâṇa* has become controlled, then we shall immediately find that all the other actions of the *Prâṇa* in the body will slowly come under control. I myself have seen men who have controlled almost every muscle of the body; and why not? If I have control over certain muscles, why not over every muscle and nerve of the body? What impossibility is there? At present the control is lost, and the motion has become automatic. We cannot move the ears at will, but we know that animals can. We have not that power because we do not exercise it. This is what is called atavism.

Again, we know that motion which has become latent can be brought back to manifestation. By hard work and practice certain motions of the body which are most dormant can be brought back under perfect control. Reasoning in that way we find there is no impossibility, but, on the other hand, every probability that each part of the body can be brought under perfect control. This the *Yogî* does through *Prâṇâyâma.* Perhaps some of you have read in these books that in *Prâṇâyâma*, when drawing in the breath, you must fill your whole body with *Prâṇa.* In the English translations *Prâṇa* is given as breath, and you are inclined to ask how that is to be done. The fault is with the translator. Every part of the body can be filled with *Prâṇa.* this vital force, and when you are able to do that, you can control the whole body. All the sickness and misery felt in the body will be perfectly controlled, and, not only so, you will be able to control another's body. Everything is infectious in this world, good or bad. If your body be in a certain state of tension, it will have a tendency to produce the same tension in others. If you are strong and healthy, those that live near you will also have the tendency to become strong and healthy, but, if you are sick and weak, those around you will have the tendency to become the same. This vibration will be, as it were, conveyed to another body. In the case of one man trying to heal another, the first idea is simply transferring his own health to the other. This is the primitive sort of healing. Consciously, or unconsciously health can be transmitted. The very strong man, living with the weak man, will make him a little stronger, whether he knows it or not. When consciously done it becomes quicker and better in its action. Next come those cases in which a man may not be very healthy himself, yet we know that he can bring health to another. The first man, in such a case, has a little more control over the *Prâṇa*, and can rouse, for the time being, his *Prâṇa*, as it were, to a certain state of vibration, and transmit it to another person.

There have been cases where this process has been carried on at a distance, but in reality there is no distance, in the sense of a break. Where is the distance that has a break? Is there any break between you and the sun? It is a continuous mass of matter, the sun the one part, and you the other. Is there a break between one part of a river and another? Then why cannot any force travel? There is no reason against it. These cases are perfectly true, and this *Prâṇa* can be transmitted to a very great distance; but to one genuine case, there are hundreds of frauds. It is not so easy as it is thought to be. In the most ordinary cases of this healing you will find that these healers are simply taking advantage of the naturally healthy state of the human body. There is no disease in this world which kills the majority of persons attacked. Even in cholera epidemics, if for a few days sixty per cent. die, after that the rate comes down to thirty and twenty per cent, and the rest recover. An allopath comes and treats cholera patients, and gives them his medicines; the homœopath comes and gives his medicine, and cures perhaps more, simply because the homœopath did not disturb the patients, but allowed nature to deal with them; and the faith-healer will cure more still, because he will bring the strength of his mind to bear, and rouses, through faith, the dormant *Prâṇa* of the patient.

But there is a mistake constantly made by faith-healers; they think that it is faith itself that directly heals a man. It alone will not cover all the ground. There are diseases where the worst symptoms are that the patient never thinks that he has that disease. That tremendous faith of the patient is itself one symptom of the disease, and usually indicates that he will die quickly. In such cases the principle that faith cures does not apply. If it were faith that cured in all these cases, these patients also would be cured. It is by this *Prâṇa* that real curing comes. The pure man, who has controlled this *Prâṇa*, has the power of bringing it into a certain state of vibration, which can be conveyed to others, arousing in them a similar vibration. You see that in every-day actions. I am talking to you. What am I trying to do? I am, so to say, bringing my mind to a certain state of vibration, and the more I succeed in bringing it to that state, the more you will be affected by what I say. All of you know that the day I am more enthusiastic the more you enjoy the lecture, and when I am less enthusiastic you feel lack of interest.

The gigantic will powers of the world, the world-movers, can bring their *Prâṇa* into a high state of vibration, and it is so great and powerful that it catches others in a moment, and thousands are drawn towards them, and half the world thinks as they do. Great prophets of the world had the most wonderful control of this *Prâṇa*, which gave them tremendous will power; they had brought their *Prâṇa* to the highest state of motion, and this is what gave them power to sway the world. All manifestations of power arise from this control. Men may not know the secret, but this is the one explanation. Sometimes in your own body the supply of *Prâṇa* gravitates more or less to one part; the balance is disturbed, and when the balance of *Prâṇa* is disturbed, what we call disease is produced. To take away the superfluous *Prâṇa*, or to supply the *Prâṇa* that is wanting, will be curing the disease. That again is *Prâṇâyâma*, to learn when there is more or less *Prâṇa* in one part of the body than there should be. The feelings will become so subtle that the mind will feel that there is less *Prâṇa* in the toe or the finger than there should be, and possess the power to supply it. These are among the various functions of *Prâṇâyâma*. They have to be learned slowly and gradually, and, as you see, the whole scope of *Râja Yoga* is really to teach the control and direction in different planes of the *Prâṇa*. When a man has concentrated his energies he masters the *Prâṇa* that is in his body. When a man is meditating, he is also concentrating the *Prâṇa*.

In an ocean there are huge waves, like mountains, then smaller waves, and still smaller, down to little bubbles, but the background of all these is the infinite ocean. The bubble is connected with the infinite ocean at one end, and the huge wave at the other end. So, one may be a gigantic man, and another a little bubble, but each is connected with that infinite ocean of energy, and this is the common birthright of every animal that exists. Wherever there is life, the storehouse of infinite energy is behind it. Starting from some fungus, some very minute, microscopic bubble, and all the time drawing from that infinite storehouse of energy, the form is changed slowly and slowly, until, in course of time it becomes a plant, then an animal, then man, ultimately God. This is attained through millions of æons, but what is time? An increase of speed, an increase of struggle, is able to bridge the distance of time. That which naturally takes a long time to accomplish can be shortened by the intensity of the action, says the *Yogî*. A man may go on slowly drawing in this energy from the infinite mass that exists in the universe, and perhaps he will require a hundred thousand years to become a Deva, and then, perhaps, five hundred thousand years to become still higher, and perhaps five millions of years to become perfect. Given rapid growth the time will be lessened. Why is it not possible, with sufficient effort, to reach this very perfection in six months or six years? There is no limit. Reason shows that. If an engine, with a certain amount of coal, runs at two miles an hour, add more coal, and it will run in quicker time. Similarly why shall not the soul, by intensifying its action, attain to that goal in this very life? All beings will at last attain to that perfection we know. But who cares to wait all these millions of æons? Why not reach it immediately, in this body even, in this human form?

Why shall I not get that infinite knowledge, infinite power now?

That is the ideal of the *Yogî*; the whole science of *Yoga* is directed to that one end, to teach men how to shorten the time by adding power, how to intensify the power of assimilation, and thereby shorten the time for reaching perfection, instead of slowly advancing from point to point, and waiting until the whole human race has come out, and become perfect. All the great prophets, saints, and seers, of the world, what are they? In that one span of life they lived the whole life of humanity, bridged the whole length of time that it will take ordinary humanity to come to the state of perfection. In this life they perfect themselves; they have no thought for anything else, breathe for nothing else, never live a moment for any other idea, and thus the way is shortened for them. This is what is meant by concentration, intensifying the action or assimilation, and thus shortening the time; and *Râja Yoga* is the science which teaches us how to gain the power of concentration.

What has this *Prâṇâyâma* to do with spiritualism? That is also a manifestation of *Prâṇâyâma*. If it be true that the departed spirits exist, only that we cannot see them, it is quite probable that there may be hundreds and millions living here that we can neither see, feel, nor touch. We may be continually passing and repassing through their bodies, and it is also probable that they do not see or feel us. It is a circle within a circle, universe within universe. Those only that are on the same plane see each other. We have five senses, and we represent *Prâṇa* in a certain state of vibration. All beings in the same state of vibration will see each other, but if there are beings who represent *Prâṇa* in a higher state of vibration they will not be seen. We may increase the intensity of light until we cannot see the light at all, but there may be beings with eyes so powerful that they can see such light. Again, if the vibrations are very low, we do not see light, but there are animals that see it, as cats and owls. Our range of vision is only one plane of the vibrations of this *Prâṇa*. Take this atmosphere, for instance; it is piled up layer on layer, but the layers nearer to the earth are denser than those above and as you go higher the atmosphere becomes finer and finer. Or take the case of the ocean; as you go deeper and deeper the density of the water increases, and those animals that live at the bottom of the sea can never come up, or they will be broken into pieces.

Think of this whole universe as an ocean of ether, in vibration under the action of *Prâṇa*, and that it consists of layer after layer of varying degrees of vibration; in the more external the vibrations are less, and nearer to the centre the vibrations become quicker and quicker, and each range of vibration makes one plane. Think of the whole thing as one circle, the centre of which is perfection; the further you get from the centre the slower the vibrations. Matter is the outermost crust, next comes mind, and spirit is the centre. Then suppose these ranges of vision are cut into planes, so many millions of miles one set of vibration, and then so many millions of miles still higher, and so on. It is perfectly certain, then, that those who live on the plane of a certain state of vibration will have the power of recognising each other, but will not recognise those above or below them. Yet, just as by the telescope and the microscope we can increase the scope of our vision, and make higher or lower vibrations cognisable to us, similarly, every man can bring himself to the state of vibration belonging to the next plane, thus enabling himself to see what is going on there. Suppose this room were full of beings whom we do not see. They represent certain vibrations in the *Prâṇa*, and we represent other vibrations. Suppose they represent the quicker, and we the slower. *Prâṇa* is the material of which they are composed, also of which we are composed; all are parts of the same ocean of *Prâṇa*, only the rate of vibration differs. If I can bring myself to the quicker vibration this plane will immediately change for me; I shall not see you any more; you vanish, and they appear. Some of you, perhaps, know this to be true. All this bringing of the mind into a higher state of vibration is included in one word in *Yoga* — *Samâdhi*. All these states of higher vibration, superconscious vibrations of the mind, are grouped in that one word, *Samâdhi*, and the lower states of *Samâdhi* give us visions of these beings. The highest grade of *Samâdhi* is when we see the real thing, when we see the material out of which the whole of these grades of beings are composed, and that lump of clay being known, we know all the clay in the universe.

Thus we see that this *Prâṇâyâma* includes all that is true of spiritualism even. Similarly, you will find that wherever any sect or body of people is trying to search out anything occult and mystical, or hidden, it is really this *Yoga*, this attempt to control the *Prâṇa*. You will find that wherever there is any extraordinary display of power it is the manifestation of this *Prâṇa*. Even the physical sciences can be included also in *Prâṇâyâma*. What moves the steam engine? *Prâṇa*, acting through the steam. What are all these phenomena of electricity and so forth but *Prâṇa*? What is physical science? *Prâṇâyâma*, by external means. *Prâṇa*, manifesting itself as mental power, can only be controlled by mental means. That part of the *Prâṇâyâma* which attempts to control the physical manifestations of the *Prâṇa* by physical means is called physical science, and that part which tries to control the manifestations of the *Prâṇa* as mental force, by mental means, is called *Râja Yoga*.

CHAPTER IV.

THE PSYCHIC PRÂṆA.

ACCORDING to the *Yogîs* there are two nerve currents in the spinal column, called *Pingalâ* and *Iḍâ*, and there is a hollow canal called *Suṣumnâ* running through the spinal cord. At the lower end of the hollow canal is what the *Yogîs* call the "Lotus of the *Kuṇḍalinî*." They describe it as triangular in form, in which, in the symbolical language of the *Yogîs*, there is a power called the *Kuṇḍalinî* coiled up. When that *Kuṇḍalinî* awakes it tries to force a passage through this hollow canal, and, as it rises step by step, as it were, layer after layer of the mind becomes open, all these different visions and wonderful powers come to the *Yogî*. When it reaches the brain the *Yogî* is perfectly detached from the body and mind; the soul finds itself free. We know that the spinal cord is composed in a peculiar manner. If we take the figure eight horizontally (∞) there are two parts, and these two parts are connected in the middle. Suppose you add eight after eight, piled one on top of the other, that will represent the spinal cord. The left is the *Iḍâ*, and the right the *Pingalâ*, and that hollow canal which runs through the centre of the spinal cord is the *Suṣumnâ*. Where the spinal cord ends in some of the lumbar vertebræ, a fine fibre comes down, and the canal is even in that fibre, only much finer. The canal is closed at the lower end, which is situated near what is called the sacral plexus, which, according to modern physiology, is triangular in form. The different plexuses that have their centres in the spinal cord can very well stand for the different "lotuses" of the *Yogî*.

The *Yogî* conceives of several centres, beginning with the *Mûlâdhâra*, the basic, and ending with the *Sahaśrâra*, the thousand-petalled lotus in the brain. So, if we take these different plexuses as representing these circles, the idea of the *Yogî* can be understood very easily in the language of modern physiology. We know there are two sorts of actions in these nerve currents, one afferent, the other efferent, one sensory and the other motor; one centripetal, and the other centrifugal. One carries the sensations to the brain, and the other from the brain to the outer body. These vibrations are all connected with the brain in the long run. Several other facts we have to remember, in order to clear the way for the explanation which is to come. This spinal cord, at the brain, ends in a sort of bulb, in the medulla, which is not attached to the bone, but floats in a fluid in the brain, so that if there be a blow on the head the force of that blow will be dissipated in the fluid, and will not hurt the bulb. This will be an important fact as we go on. Secondly, we have also to know that, of all the centres, we have particularly to remember three, the *Mûlâdhâra* (the basic), the *Sahaśrâra* (the thousand-petalled lotus of the brain) and the *Svâdhiṣṭhâna* (next above the *Mûlâdhâra*). Next we will take one fact from physics. We all hear of electricity, and various other forces connected with it. What electricity is no one knows, but, so far as it is known, it is a sort of motion.

There are various other motions in the universe; what is the difference between them and electricity? Suppose this table moves, that the molecules which compose this table are moving in different directions; if they are all made to move in the same direction it will be electricity. Electric motion is when the molecules all move in the same direction. If all the air molecules in a room are made to move in the same direction it will make a gigantic battery of electricity of the room. Another point from physiology we must remember, that the centre which regulates the respiratory system, the breathing system, has a sort of controlling action over the system of nerve currents, and the controlling centre of the respiratory system is opposite the thorax, in the spinal column. This centre regulates the respiratory organs, and also exercises some control over the secondary centres.

Now we shall see why breathing is practised. In the first place, from rhythmical breathing will come a tendency of all the molecules in the body to have the same direction. When mind changes into will, the currents change into a motion similar to electricity, because the nerves have been proved to show polarity under action of electric currents. This shows that when the will evolves into the nerve currents it is changed into something like electricity. When all the motions of the body have become perfectly rhythmical the body has, as it were, become a gigantic battery of will. This tremendous will is exactly what the *Yogî* wants. This is, therefore, a physiological explanation of the breathing exercise. It tends to bring a rhythmic action in the body, and helps us, through the respiratory centre, to control the other centres. The aim of *Prâṇâyâma* here is to rouse the coiled-up power in the *Mûlâdhâra*, called the *Kuṇḍalinî*.

Everything that we see, or imagine, or dream, we have to perceive in space. This is the ordinary space, called the *Mahâkâśa*, or great space. When a *Yogî* reads the thoughts of other men, or perceives supersensuous objects, he sees them in another sort of space called the *Chittâkâśa*, the mental space. When perception has become objectless, and the soul shines in its own nature, it is called the *Chidâkâśa*, or knowledge space. When the *Kuṇḍalinî* is aroused, and enters the canal of the *Suṣumnâ* all the perceptions are in the mental space. When it has reached that end of the canal which opens out into the brain, the objectless perception is in the knowledge space. Taking the analogy of electricity, we find that man can send a current only along a wire, but nature requires no wires to send her tremendous currents. This proves that the wire is not really necessary, but that only our inability to dispense with it compels us to use it.

Similarly, all the sensations and motions of the body are being sent into the brain, and sent out of it, through these wires of nerve fibres. The columns of sensory and motor fibres in the spinal cord are the *Iḍâ* and *Pingalâ* of the *Yogîs*. They are the main channels through which the afferent and efferent currents are travelling. But why should not the mind send the news without any wire, or react without any wires? We see that this is being done in nature. The *Yogî* says if you can do that you have got rid of the bondage of matter. How to do it? If you can make the current pass through the *Suṣumnâ*, the canal in the middle of the spinal column, you have solved the problem. The mind has made this net-work of the nervous system, and has to break it, so that no wires will be required to work through. Then alone will all knowledge come to us—no more bondage of body; that is why it is so important that you should get control of that *Suṣumnâ*. If you can send the mental current through that hollow canal without any nerve fibres to act as wires, the *Yogî* says you have solved the problem, and he also says it can be done.

This *Suṣumnâ* is, in ordinary persons, closed up at the lower extremity; no action comes through it. The *Yogî* proposes a practice by which it can be opened, and the nerve currents made to travel through. When a sensation is carried to a centre, the centre reacts. This reaction, in the case of automatic centres, is followed by motion; in the case of conscious centres it is followed first by perception, and secondly by motion. All perception is the reaction to action from outside. How, then, do perceptions in dreams arise? There is then no action from outside. The sensory motions, therefore, are coiled up somewhere, just as the motor motions are known to be in different centres. For instance, I see a city; the perception of that city was from the reaction to the sensations brought from outside objects comprising that city. That is to say, a certain motion in the brain molecules has been set up by the motion in the incarrying nerves, which again were set in motion by external objects in the city. Now, even after a long time I can remember the city. This memory is exactly the same phenomenon, only it is in a milder form. But whence is the action that set up even the milder form of similar vibrations in the brain. Not certainly from the primary sensations. Therefore it must be that the sensations are coiled up somewhere, and they, by their acting, bring out the mild reaction which we call dream perception. Now the centre where all these residual sensations are, as it were, stored up, is called the *Mûlâdhâra*, the root receptacle, and the coiled up energy of action is *Kuṇḍalinî*, the "coiled up." It is very probable that the residual motor energy is also stored up in the same centre as, after deep study or meditation on external objects, the part of the body where the *Mûlâdhâra* centre is situated (probably the sacral plexus) gets heated. Now, if this coiled-up energy be roused and made active, and then consciously made to travel up the *Suśumnâ* canal, as it acts upon centre after centre, a tremendous reaction will set in. When a minute portion of the energy of action travels along a nerve fibre and causes reaction from centres, the perception is either dream or imagination. But when the vast mass of this energy stored up by the power of long internal meditation travels along the *Suṣumnâ*, and strikes the centres, the reaction is tremendous, immensely superior to the reaction of dream or imagination, immensely more intense than the reaction of sense perception. It is super-sensuous perception, and the mind in that state is called superconscious. And when it reaches the metropolis of all sensations, the brain, the whole brain, as it were, reacts, and every perceiving molecule in the body, as it were, reacts, and the result is the full blaze of illumination, the perception of the Self. As this *Kuṇḍalinî* force travels from centre to centre, layer after layer of the mind, as it were, will be opened up, and this universe will be perceived by the *Yogî* in its fine, or coarse, form. Then alone the causes of this universe, both as sensation and reaction, will be known as they are, and hence will come all knowledge. The causes being known, the knowledge of the effects is sure to follow.

Thus the rousing of the *Kuṇḍalinî* is the one and only way to attaining Divine Wisdom, and super-conscious perception, the realisation of the spirit. It may come in various ways, through love for God, through the mercy of perfected sages, or through the power of the analytic will of the philosopher. Wherever there is any manifestation of what is ordinarily called supernatural power or wisdom, there must have been a little current of *Kuṇḍalinî* which found its way into the *Suṣumnâ*. Only, in the vast majority of such cases of super-naturalism, they had ignorantly stumbled on to some practice which set free a minute portion of the coiled-up *Kuṇḍalinî*. All worship, consciously or unconsciously, leads to this end. The man who thinks that he is receiving responses to his prayers does not know that the fulfilment came only from his own nature, that he has succeeded by the mental attitude of prayer in waking up a bit of this infinite power which is coiled up within himself. Whom, thus, men ignorantly worship under various names, through fear and tribulation, the *Yogî* declares to the world to be the real power coiled up in every being, the mother of eternal happiness, if we know how to approach her. And *Râja Yoga* is the science of religion, the rationale of all worship, all prayers, forms, ceremonies, and miracles.

CHAPTER V.

THE CONTROL OF PSYCHIC PRÂṆA.

We have now to deal with the exercises in *Prâṇâyâma*. We have seen that the first step will be, according to the *Yogîs*, to control the motion of the lungs. What we want to do is to feel the finer motions that are going on in the body. Our minds have become externalised, and have lost sight of the fine motions inside. If we can begin to feel them, we can begin to control them. These nerve currents are going on all over the body, bringing life and vitality to every muscle, but we do not feel them. The *Yogî* says we can learn to do so. How? By taking up and controlling all these motions of the *Prâṇa* beginning with the motion of the lungs, and when we have done that for a sufficient length of time we shall also be able to control the finer motions.

We now come to the exercises in *Prâṇâyâma*. Sit upright; the body must be kept straight. The spinal cord, although it is inside the vertebral column, is not attached to it. If you sit crookedly you disturb this spinal cord, so let it be free. Any time that you sit crookedly and try to meditate you are doing yourself an injury. The three parts of the body must be always held straight, the chest, the neck, and the head, in one line. You will find that by a little practice this will come to you just as breathing. The second thing is to get control of the nerves. We have seen that the nerve centre that controls the respiratory organs, has a sort of controlling effect on the other nerves, and rhythmical breathing is therefore necessary. The breathing that we generally use should not be called breathing at all. It is very irregular. Then there are some natural differences of breathing between men and women.

The first lesson is just to breathe in a measured way, in and out. That will harmonise the system. When you have practised this for some time you will do well to join the repetition of some word to it, as "*Om*," or any other sacred word, and let the word flow in and out with the breath, rhythmically, harmoniously, and you will find the whole body is becoming rhythmical. Then you will learn what rest is. Sleep is not rest, comparatively. Once this rest has come the most tired nerves will be calmed down, and you will find that you have never before really rested. In India we use certain symbolical words instead of counting one, two, three, four. That is why I advise you to join the mental repetition of the "*Om*," or other sacred word to the *Prâṇâyâma*.

The first effect of this practice will be that the face will change; harsh lines will disappear; with this calm thought calmness will come over the face. Next, beautiful voice will come. I never saw a *Yogî* with a croaking voice. These signs will come after a few months' practice. After practising this first breathing for a few days, you take up a higher one. Slowly fill the lungs with breath through the *Iḍâ*, the left nostril, and at the same time concentrate the mind on the nerve current. You are, as it were, sending the nerve current down the spinal column, and striking violently on that last plexus, the basic lotus, which is triangular in form, the seat of the *Kuṇḍalinî*. Then hold the current there for some time. Imagine that you are slowly drawing that nerve current with the breath through the other side, then slowly throw it out through the right nostril. This you will find a little difficult to practise. The easiest way is to stop the right nostril with the thumb, and then slowly draw in the breath through the left; then close both nostrils with thumb and forefinger, and imagine that you are sending that current down, and striking the base of the *Suṣumnâ*; then take the thumb off, and let the breath out through the right nostril. Next inhale slowly through that nostril, keeping the other closed by the forefinger, then close both, as before. The way the Hindûs practise this would be very difficult for this country, because they do it from their childhood, and their lungs are prepared for it. Here it is well to begin with four seconds, and slowly increase. Draw in four seconds, hold in sixteen seconds, then throw out in eight seconds. This makes one *Prâṇâyâma*. At the same time think of the triangle, concentrate the mind on that centre. The imagination can help you a great deal. The next breathing is slowly drawing the breath in, and then immediately throwing it out slowly, and then stopping the breath out, using the same numbers. The only difference is that in the first case the breath was held in, and in the second, held out. The last is the easier one. The breathing in which you hold the breath in the lungs must not be practised too much. Do it only four times in the morning, and four times in the evening. Then you can slowly increase the time and number. You will find that you have the power to do so, and that you take pleasure in it. So, very carefully and cautiously increase as you feel that you have the power, to six instead of four. It may injure you if you practise it irregularly.

Of the three processes, the purification of the nerves, the retaining the breath inside and the keeping the breath outside, the first and the last are neither difficult nor dangerous. The more you practise the first one the calmer you will be. Just think of "*Om*," and you can practise even while you are sitting at your work. You will be all the better for it. One day, if you practise hard the *Kuṇḍalinî* will be aroused. For those who practise once or twice a day, just a little calmness of the body and mind will come, and beautiful voice; only for those who can go on further with it will this *Kuṇḍalinî* be aroused, and the whole of this nature will begin to change, and the book of knowledge will be open. No more will you need to go to books for knowledge; your own mind will have become your book, containing infinite knowledge. I have already spoken of the *Iḍâ* and *Pingalâ* currents, flowing through either side of the spinal column, also of the *Suṣumnâ*, the passage through the centre of the spinal cord. These three are present in every animal; whatever has a spinal column has these three lines of action, but the *Yogîs* claim that in ordinary mankind the *Suṣumnâ* is closed, that action there is not evident, while in the other two it is evident, carrying power to different parts of the body.

The *Yogî* alone has the *Suṣumnâ* open. When this *Suṣumnâ* current opens, and thought begins to rise through it, we get beyond the senses, our minds become supersensuous, superconscious, we get beyond even the intellect, and where reasoning cannot reach. To open that *Suṣumnâ* is the prime object of the *Yogî*. According to him, along this *Suṣumnâ* are ranged these centres of distribution, or, in more figurative language, these lotuses, as they are called. The lowest one is at the lowest end of the spinal cord, and is called *Mûlâdhâra*, the next one is called *Svâdhiṣṭhâna*, the next *Manipûra*, the next *Anâhata*, the next *Viśuddha*, the next *Ajna*, and the last, which is in the brain, is the *Sahaśrâra*, or "the thousand petalled." Of these we have to take cognition just now of only two centres, the lowest, the *Mûlâdhâra*, and the highest, the *Sahaśrâra*. The lowest one is where all energy becomes stored up, and that energy has to be taken up from there and brought to the last one, the brain. The *Yogîs* claim that of all the energies that the human body comprises the highest is what they call "*Ojas*." Now this *Ojas* is stored up in the brain, and the more the *Ojas* is in a man's head, the more powerful he is, the more intellectual, the more spiritually strong will that man be. This is the action of *Ojas*. One man may speak beautiful language and beautiful thoughts, but they do not impress people; another man speaks neither beautiful language nor beautiful thoughts, yet his words charm. That is the power of *Ojas* coming out. Every movement coming from him will be powerful.

Now in all mankind there is more or less of this *Ojas* stored up. And all the forces that are working in the body, in their highest form, become *Ojas*. You must remember that it is only a question of transformation. The same force which is working outside, as electricity or magnetism, will become changed into inner force; the same forces that are working as muscular energy will be changed into *Ojas*. The *Yogîs* say that that part of the human energy which is expressed as sex energy, in sexual functions, sexual thought, and so on, when checked and controlled, easily becomes changed into *Ojas*, and as this lowest centre is the one which guides all these functions, therefore the *Yogî* pays particular attention to that centre. He tries to take up all this sexual energy and convert it into *Ojas*. It is only the chaste man or woman who can make the *Ojas* rise and become stored in the brain, and that is why chastity has always been considered the highest virtue, because man feels that if he is unchaste, spirituality goes away, he loses mental vigour, and strong moral stamina. That is why in all of the religious orders in the world that have produced spiritual giants you will always find this intense chastity insisted upon. That is why the monks came into existence, giving up marriage. There must be perfect chastity, in thought, word and deed. Without it the practice of *Râja Yoga* is dangerous, and may lead to insanity. If people practise *Râja Yoga* and at the same time lead an impure life, how can they expect to become *Yogîs?*

CHAPTER VI.

PRATYÂHÂRA AND DHÂRAṆÂ.

THE next step is called *Pratyâhâra*. What is this? You know how perceptions come. First of all there are the external instruments, then the internal organs, acting in the body through the brain centres, and there is the mind. When these come together, and attach themselves to some external thing, then we perceive that thing. At the same time it is a very difficult thing to concentrate the mind and attach it to one organ only; the mind is a slave.

We hear "be good" and "be good" and "be good" taught all over the world. There is hardly a child, born in any country in the world, who has not been told "do not steal," "do not tell a lie," but nobody tells the child how he can help it. Talking will never do it. Why should he not become a thief? We do not teach him how not to steal; we simply tell him "do not steal." Only when we teach him to control his mind do we really help him. All actions, internal and external, occur when the mind joins itself to certain centres, which centres are called the organs. Willingly or unwillingly it is drawn to join itself to the centres, and that is why people do foolish deeds and feel misery, which, if the mind were under control, they would not do. What would be the result of controlling the mind? It then would not join itself to the centres of perception, and, naturally, feeling and willing would be under control. It is clear so far. Is it possible? It is perfectly possible. You see it in modern times; the faith-healers teach people to deny misery and pain and evil. Their philosophy is rather roundabout, but it is a part of *Yoga* into which they have somehow stumbled. In those cases where they succeed in making a person throw off suffering by denying it they have really taught a part of *Pratyâhâra*, as they have made the mind of the person taught strong enough to refuse to take up the record of the senses. The hypnotists in a similar manner, by their suggestion, excite in the patient a sort of morbid *Pratyâhâra* for the time being. The so-called hypnotic suggestion can only act upon a diseased body and a clouded mind. And until the operator, by means of fixed gaze or otherwise, has succeeded in putting the mind of the subject in a sort of passive, morbid condition, his suggestions never work.

Now the control of the centres which is established in a hypnotic patient or the patient of faith-healing, for a time, is utterly reprehensible, because it leads to ultimate ruin. It is not really controlling the brain centres by the power of one's own will, but is, as it were, stunning the patient's mind for a time by sudden blows which another's will delivers to it. It is not checking by means of reins and muscular strength the mad career of a fiery team, but rather by asking another to deliver heavy blows on the heads of the horses, to stun them for a time into gentleness. At each one of these processes the man operated upon loses a part of his mental energies, and, at last, the mind, instead of gaining the power of perfect control, becomes a shapeless, powerless mass, and the only goal of the patient is the lunatic asylum.

Every attempt at control which is not voluntary, not with the controller's own mind, is not only disastrous, but it defeats the end. The goal of each soul is freedom, mastery, freedom from the slavery of matter and thought, mastery of external and internal nature. Instead of leading towards that, every will current from another, in whatever form it comes to me, either as direct control of my organs, or as forcing me to control them while under a morbid condition, only rivets one link more to the already existing heavy chain of bondage of past thoughts, past superstition. Therefore, beware how you allow yourselves to be acted upon by others. Beware how you unknowingly bring another to ruin. True, some succeed in doing good to many for a time, by giving a new trend to their propensities, but at the same time, they bring ruin to millions by the unconscious hypnotic suggestions they throw around, rousing in men and women that morbid, passive, hypnotic condition which makes them almost soulless at last. Whosoever, therefore, asks anyone to believe blindly, or drags mankind behind him through controlling it by his superior will is an injurer to humanity, though he may not have intended it.

Therefore use your own minds, control body and

mind yourselves, remember that until you are a diseased person, no extraneous will can work upon you, and avoid everyone, however great and good he may be, who asks you to blindly believe. All over the world there have been dancing, and jumping, and howling sects, who spread like infections when they begin to sing and dance and preach; they also come under this heading. They exercise a singular control for the time being over sensitive persons, alas, often, in the long run, to degenerate whole races. Aye, it is healthier for the individual or the race to remain wicked than to be made apparently good by such morbid extraneous control. One's heart sinks to think of the amount of injury done to humanity by such irresponsible, yet well-meaning religious fanatics. They little know that the minds which attain to sudden spiritual upheaval under their suggestions, with music and prayers, are simply making themselves passive, morbid, and powerless, and opening themselves to any other suggestion, be it ever so evil. Little do these ignorant, deluded persons dream that whilst they are congratulating themselves upon their miraculous power to transform human hearts, which power they think was poured upon them by some Being above the clouds, they are sowing the seeds of future decay, of crime, of lunacy, and of death. Therefore, beware of everything that takes away your freedom. Know that it is dangerous, and avoid it by all the means in your power. He who has succeeded in attaching or detaching his mind to or from the centres at will has succeeded in *Pratyâhâra*, which means "gathering towards," checking the outgoing powers of the mind, freeing it from the thraldom of the senses. When we can do this we shall really possess a character; then alone we shall have made a long step towards freedom; before that we are mere machines.

How hard it is to control the mind. Well has it been compared to the maddened monkey. There was a monkey, restless by his own nature, as all monkeys are. As if that were not enough someone made him drink freely of wine, so that he became still more restless. Then a scorpion stung him. When a man is stung by a scorpion he jumps about for a whole day, so the poor monkey found his condition worse than ever. To complete his misery a demon entered into him. What language can describe the uncontrollable restlessness of that monkey? The human mind is like that monkey; incessantly active by its own nature, then it becomes drunk with the wine of desire, thus increasing its turbulence. After desire takes possession comes the sting of the scorpion of jealousy of others whose desires meet with fulfilment, and last of all the demon of pride takes possession of the mind, making it think itself of all importance. How hard to control such a mind.

The first lesson, then, is to sit for some time and let the mind run on. The mind is bubbling up all the time. It is like that monkey jumping about. Let the monkey jump as much as he can; you simply wait and watch. Knowledge is power says the proverb, and that is true. Until you know what the mind is doing you cannot control it. Give it the full length of the reins; many most hideous thoughts may come into it; you will be astonished that it was possible for you to think such thoughts. But you will find that each day the mind's vagaries are becoming less and less violent, that each day it is becoming calmer. In the first few months you will find that the mind will have a thousand thoughts, later you will find that it is toned down to perhaps seven hundred, and after a few more months it will have fewer and fewer, until at last it will be under perfect control, but we must patiently practise every day. As soon as the steam is turned on the engine must run, and as soon as things are before us we must perceive; so a man, to prove that he is not a machine, must demonstrate that he is under the control of nothing. This controlling of the mind, and not allowing it to join itself to the centres, is *Pratyâhâra*. How is this practised? It is a long work, not to be done in a day. Only after a patient, continuous struggle for years can we succeed.

The next lesson depends on this. After you have practised the *Pratyâhâra* for a time, take the next step, the *Dhâraṇâ*, holding the mind to certain points. What is meant by holding the mind to certain points? Forcing the mind to feel certain parts of the body to the exclusion of others. For instance, try to feel only the hand, to the exclusion of other parts of the body. When the *Chitta*, or mind-stuff, is confined and limited to a certain place, this is called *Dhâraṇâ*. This *Dhâraṇâ* is of various sorts, and along with it, it is better to have a little play of the imagination. For instance, the mind should be made to think of one point in the heart. That is very difficult; an easier way is to imagine a lotus there. That lotus is full of light, effulgent light. Put the mind there. Or think of the lotus in the brain as full of light, or of the different centres in the *Suṣumnâ* mentioned before.

The *Yogî* must always practise. He should try to live alone; the companionship of different sorts of people distracts his mind; he should not speak much, because to speak distracts the mind; nor work much, because too much work distracts the mind; the mind cannot be controlled after a whole day's hard work. One with such a determination becomes a *Yogî*. Such is the power of good that even the least done will bring a great amount of benefit. It will not hurt anyone, but will benefit everyone. First of all it will tone down nervous excitement, bring calmness, enable us to see things more clearly. The temperament will be better, and the health will be better. Sound health will be one of the first signs, and a beautiful voice. Defects in the voice will be changed. This will be among the first of the many effects that will come. Those who practise hard will get many other signs. Sometimes there will be sounds, as a peal of bells heard at a distance, commingling, and falling on the ear as one continuous sound. Sometimes things will be seen, little specks of light floating and becoming bigger and bigger, and when these things come, know that you are progressing very fast. Those who want to be *Yogîs*, and practise very hard, must take a little care of their diet at first. Those who want to make very rapid progress, if they can live on milk alone for some months, and cereals, will find it an advantage. But for those who want only a little practice for every day business sort of life, let them not eat too much, but otherwise they may eat whatever they please.

For those who want to make faster progress, and to practise hard, a strict diet is absolutely necessary. As the organisation becomes finer and finer, at first you will find that the least thing throws you out of balance. One bit of food more or less will disturb the whole system, until you get perfect control, and then you will be able to eat whatever you like. You will find that when you are beginning to concentrate, the dropping of a pin will seem like a thunderbolt going through your brain. The organs get finer, and the perceptions get finer. These are the stages through which we have to pass, and all those who persevere will succeed. Give up all argumentation and other distractions. Is there anything in this dry intellectual jargon? It only throws the mind off its balance and disturbs it. These things have to be realised. Will talking do that? So give up all vain talk. Read only those books which have been written by persons who have had realisation

Be like the pearl oyster. There is a pretty Indian fable to the effect that if it rains when the star *Svâtî* is in the ascendant, and a drop of rain falls into an oyster, that drop will become a pearl. The oysters know this, so they come to the surface when that star shines, and wait to catch the precious rain-drop. When one falls into the shell, quickly the oyster closes it and dives down to the bottom of the sea, there to patiently develop the drop into the pearl. We should be like that. First hear, then understand, and then, leaving all distractions, shut our minds to outside influences, and devote ourselves to developing the truth within us. There is the danger of frittering away our energies by taking up an idea only for its novelty, and then giving it up for another that is newer. Take one thing up and do it, and see the end of it, and before you have seen the end, do not give it up. He who can become mad upon an idea, he alone will see light. Those that only take a nibble here and there will never attain anything. They may titillate their nerves for a moment, but there it will end. They will be slaves in the hands of nature, and will never get beyond the senses.

Those who really want to be *Yogís* must give up, once for all, this nibbling at things. Take up one idea. Make that one idea your life; dream of it; think of it; live on that idea. Let the brain, the body, muscles, nerves, every part of your body be full of that idea, and just leave every other idea alone. This is the way to success, and this is the way great spiritual giants are produced. Others are mere talking machines. If we really want to be blessed, and make others blessed, we must go deeper, and, for the first step, do not disturb the mind, and do not associate with persons whose ideas are disturbing. All of you know that certain persons, certain places, certain foods, repel you. Avoid them; and those who want to go to the highest, must avoid all company, good or bad. Practise hard; whether you live or die it does not matter. You have to plunge in and work, without thinking of the result. If you are brave enough, in six months you will be a perfect *Yogî*. But, for others, those who take up just a bit of it, a little of everything, they get no higher. It is of no use to simply take a course of lessons. Those who are full of *Tamas*, ignorant and dull, those whose minds never get fixed on any idea, who only crave for something to entertain them — religion and philosophy are simply entertainments to them. They come to religion as to an entertainment, and get that little bit of entertainment. These are the unpersevering. They hear a talk, think it very nice, and then go home and forget all about it. To succeed, you must have tremendous perseverance, tremendous will. "I will drink the ocean," says the persevering soul. "At my will mountains will crumble up." Have that sort of energy, that sort of will, work hard, and you will reach the goal.

CHAPTER VII.

DHYANA AND SAMÂDHI.

We have finished a cursory review of the different steps in *Râja Yoga*, except the finer ones, the training in concentration, which is the aim, the goal, to which *Râja Yoga* will lead us. We see, as human beings, that all our knowledge which is called rational is referred to consciousness. I am conscious of this table, I am conscious of your presence, and so forth, and that makes me know that you are here, and that the table is here, and things I see, feel and hear, are here. At the same time, there is a very great part of my existence of which I am not conscious — all the different organs inside the body, the different parts of the brain, the brain itself; nobody is conscious of these things.

When I eat food I do it consciously, when I assimilate it I do it unconsciously, when the food is manufactured into blood it is done unconsciously; when out of the blood all the different parts of my body are made, it is done unconsciously; and yet it is I who am doing this; there cannot be twenty people in this one body. How do I know that I do it, and nobody else? It may be urged that my business is only in eating the food, and assimilating the food, and that manufacturing the body out of the food is done for me by somebody else. That cannot be, because it can be demonstrated that almost every action of which we are unconscious now can be again brought up to the plane of consciousness. The heart is beating apparently without our control; we none of us here can control the heart; it goes on its own way. But by practice men can bring even the heart under control, until it will just beat at will, slowly, or quickly, or almost stop. Nearly every part of the body can be brought under control. What does this show? That these things which are beneath consciousness are also worked by us, only we are doing it unconsciously. We have, then, two planes in which the human mind is working. First is the conscious plane; that is to say that sort of work which is always accompanied with the feeling of egoism. Next comes the unconscious plane, the work beneath, that which is unaccompanied by the feeling of egoism. That part of mind-work which is unaccompanied with feeling of egoism is unconscious work, and that part which is accompanied with the feeling of egoism is conscious work. In the lower animals this unconscious work is called instinct. In higher animals, and in the highest of all animals, man, the second part, that which is accompanied with the feeling of egoism, prevails, and is called conscious work.

But it does not end here. There is a still higher plane upon which the mind can work. It can go beyond consciousness. Just as unconscious work is beneath consciousness, so there is another work which is above consciousness, and which, also, is not accompanied with the feeling of egoism. The feeling of egoism is only on the middle plane. When the mind is above or below that line there is no feeling of " I," and yet the mind works. When the mind goes beyond this line of self-consciousness it is called *Samâdhi*, or super-consciousness. It is above consciousness. How, for instance, do we know that a man in *Samâdhi* has not gone below his consciousness, has not degenerated, instead of going higher ? In both cases the works are unaccompanied with egoism ? The answer is, by the effects, by the results of the work, we know that which is below, and that which is above. When a man goes into deep sleep he enters a plane beneath consciousness. He works the body all the time, he breathes, he moves the body, perhaps, in his sleep, without any accompanying feeling of ego; he is unconscious, and when he returns from his sleep he is the same man who went into it. The sum-total of the knowledge which he had before he went into the sleep remains the same; it has not increased at all. No enlightenment has come. But if a man goes into *Samâdhi*, if he goes into it a fool, he comes out a sage.

What makes the difference ? From one state a man comes out the very same man that went in, and out of another state the man becomes enlightened, a sage, a prophet, a saint, his whole character changed, his life changed, illumined. These are the two effects. Now the effects being different, the causes must be different. As this illumination, with which a man comes back from

Samâdhi, is much higher than can be got from unconsciousness, or much higher than can be got by reasoning in a conscious state, it must therefore be superconsciousness, and *Samâdhi* is called the super-conscious state.

This, in short, is the idea of *Samâdhi*. What is its application ? The application is here. The field of reason, or of the conscious workings of the mind, is narrow and limited. There is a little circle within which human reason will have to move. It cannot go beyond it. Every attempt to go beyond is impossible, yet it is beyond this circle of reason that lies all that humanity holds most dear. All these questions, whether there is an immortal soul, whether there is a God, whether there is any supreme intelligence guiding this universe, are beyond the field of reason. Reason can never answer these questions. What does reason say ? It says, "I am agnostic; I do not know either yea or nay." Yet these questions are so important to us. Without a proper answer to them, human life will be impossible. All our ethical theories, all our moral attitudes, all that is good and great in human nature, has been moulded upon answers that have come from beyond that circle. It is very important, therefore, that we should have answers to these questions; without such answers human life will be impossible. If life is only a little five minutes' thing, if the universe is only a "fortuitous combination of atoms," then why should I do good to another ? Why should there be mercy, justice, or fellow feeling ? The best thing for this world would be to make hay while the sun shines, each man for himself. If there is no hope, why should I love my brother, and not cut his throat? If there is nothing beyond, if there is no freedom, but only rigorous dead laws, I should only try to make myself happy here. You will find people saying, now-a-days, that they have utilitarian grounds as the basis of all morality. What is this basis? Procuring the greatest amount of happiness to the greatest number. Why should I do this? Why should I not produce the greatest unhappiness to the greatest number, if that serves my purpose? How will utilitarians answer this question? How do you know what is right, or what is wrong? I am impelled by my desire for happiness and I fulfil it, and it is in my nature; I know nothing beyond. I have these desires, and must fulfil them; why should you complain? Whence come all these truths about human life, about morality, about the immortal soul, about God, about love and sympathy, about being good, and, above all, about being unselfish?

All ethics, all human action, and all human thought, hang upon this one idea of unselfishness; the whole idea of human life can be put in that one word, unselfishness. Why should we be unselfish? Where is the necessity, the force, the power, of my being unselfish? Why should I be? You call yourself a rational man, a utilitarian, but, if you do not show me a reason, I say you are irrational. Show me the reason why I should not be selfish, why I should not be like a brute, acting without reason? It may be good as poetry, but poetry is not reason. Show me a reason. Why shall I be unselfish, and why be good? Because Mr. and Mrs. So-and-so say so does not weigh with me. Where is the utility of my being unselfish? My utility is to be selfish, if utility means the greatest amount of happiness. I may get the greatest amount of happiness by cheating and robbing others. What is the answer? The utilitarian can never give it. The answer is that this world is only one drop in an infinite ocean, one link in an infinite chain. Where did those that preached unselfishness, and taught it to the human race, get this idea? We know it is not instinctive; the animals, which have instinct, do not know it. Neither is it reason; reason does not know anything about these ideas. Whence did they come?

We find, in studying history, one fact held in common by all the great teachers of religion the world ever had; they all claim to have got these truths from beyond, only many of them did not know what they were getting. For instance, one would say that an angel came down in the form of a human being, with wings, and said to him, "Hear, oh man, this is the message." Another says that a *Deva*, a bright being, appeared to him. Another says he dreamed that his ancestor came and told him all these things. He did not know anything beyond that. But this thing is common, that all claim either that they saw angels, or heard the voice of God, or saw some wonderful vision. All claim that this knowledge has come to them from beyond, not through their reasoning power. What does the science of *Yoga* teach? It teaches that they were right in claiming that all this knowledge came to them from beyond reasoning, but that it came from within themselves.

The *Yogî* teaches that the mind itself has a higher state of existence, beyond reason, a super-conscious state, and when the mind gets to that higher state, then this knowledge, beyond reasoning, comes to a man, metaphysical knowledge, beyond all physical knowledge. Metaphysical and transcendental knowledge comes to that man, and this state of going beyond reason, transcending ordinary human nature, sometimes may come by chance to a man who does not understand its science; he, as it were, stumbles into it. When he stumbles into it, he generally interprets it as from outside. So this explains why an inspiration, or this transcendental knowledge, may be the same in different countries, but in one country it will seem to come through an angel, and in another through a Deva, and in another through God. What does it mean? It means that the mind brought the knowledge by its own nature, and that the finding of the knowledge was interpreted according to the beliefs and education of the person through whom it came. The real fact is that these various men, as it were, stumbled into this super-conscious state.

The *Yogî* says there is a great danger in stumbling into this state. In a good many cases there is the danger of the brain being destroyed, and, as a rule, you will find that all those men, however great they were, who have stumbled into this super-conscious state, without understanding it, grope in the dark, and generally have, along with their knowledge, some quaint superstition. They open themselves to hallucinations. Mohammed claimed that the Angel Gabriel came to him in a cave one day and took him on the heavenly horse, Harak, and he visited the heavens. But, with all that, Mohammed spoke some wonderful truths. If you read the Qur'an, you find the most wonderful truths mixed with these superstitions. How will you explain it ? That man was inspired, no doubt, but that inspiration was, as it were, stumbled upon. He was not a trained *Yogi*, and did not know the reason of what he was doing. Think of the good Mohammed did to the world, and think of the great evil that has been done through his fanaticism ! Think of the millions massacred through his teachings, mothers bereft of their children, children made orphans, whole countries destroyed, millions upon millions of people killed!

So we see in studying the lives of all these great teachers that there was this danger. Yet we find, at the same time, that they were all inspired. Somehow or other they got into the super-conscious state, only whenever a prophet got into that state by simple force of emotion, just by heightening his emotional nature, he brought away from that state some truths, but also some fanaticism, some superstition which injured the world as much as the greatness of the teaching did good. To get any reason out of this mass of incongruity we call human life we have to transcend our reason, but we must do it scientifically, slowly, by regular practice, and we must cast off all superstition. We must take it up just as any other science, reason we must have to lay our foundation, we must follow reason as far as it leads, and when reason fails reason itself will show us the way to the highest plane. So whenever we hear a man say " I am inspired, "and then talk the most irrational nonsense, simply reject it. Why ? Because these three states of the mind — instinct, reason, and super-consciousness, or the unconscious, conscious, and super-conscious states — belong to one and the same mind. There are not three minds in one man, but one develops into the other. Instinct develops into reason, and reason into the transcendental consciousness; therefore one never contradicts the other. So, whenever you meet with wild statements which contradict human reason and common sense, reject them without any fear, because the real inspiration will never contradict, but will fulfil. Just as you find the great prophets saying, " I come not to destroy but to fulfil," so this inspiration always comes to fulfil reason, and is in direct harmony with reason, and whenever it contradicts reason you must know that it is not inspiration.

All the different steps in *Yoga* are intended to bring us scientifically to the super-conscious state, or *Samâdhi*. Furthermore, this is a most vital point to understand that inspiration is as much in every man's nature as it was in the ancient prophets. These prophets were not unique; they were just the same as you or I. They were great *Yogîs*. They had gained this super-consciousness, and you and I can get the same. They were not peculiar people. The very fact that one man ever reached that state will prove that it is possible for every man to do so. Not only is it possible, but every man must, eventually, get to that state, and that is religion. Experience is the only teacher we have. We may talk and reason all our lives, without ever understanding a word of truth, until we experience it ourselves. You cannot hope to make a man a surgeon by simply giving him a few books. You cannot satisfy my curiosity to see a country by showing me a map; I must have actual experience. Maps can only create a little curiosity in us to get more perfect knowledge. Beyond that, they have no value whatever. All clinging to books only degenerates the human mind. Was there ever a more horrible blasphemy than to say that all the knowledge of God is confined in this or that book? How dare men call God infinite, and yet try to compress Him into the covers of a little book! Millions of people have been killed because they did not believe what the books say, because they would not see all the knowledge of God within the covers of a book. Of course this killing and murdering has gone by, but the world is still tremendously bound up in a belief in books.

In order to reach the super-conscious state in a scientific manner we have to pass through these various steps that I have been teaching you in *Râja Yoga*. After

Pratyâhâra and *Dhâraṇâ*, which I taught you in the last lecture, we come to *Dhyâna*, meditation. When the mind has been trained to remain fixed on a certain internal or external location, there comes to it the power of, as it were, flowing in an unbroken current towards that point. This state is called *Dhyâna*. When this power of *Dhyâna* has been so much intensified as to be able to reject the external part of perception, and remain meditating only on the internal part, the meaning, that state is called *Samâdhi*. The three — *Dhâraṇâ*, *Dhyâna* and *Samâdhi* — together are called *Samyama*. That is, if the mind can first concentrate upon an object, and then is able to continue in that concentration for a length of time, and then, by continued concentration, to dwell only on the internal part of the perception of which the object was the effect, everything comes under the control of such a mind.

This meditative state is the highest state of existence. So long as there is desire no real happiness can come. It is only the contemplative, witness-like study of objects that brings to us real enjoyment and happiness. The animal has its happiness in the senses, the man in his intellect, and the God in spiritual contemplation. It is only to the soul that has attained to this contemplative state that the world has really become beautiful. To him who desires nothing, and does not mix himself up with them, the manifold changes of nature are one panorama of beauty and sublimity.

These ideas have to be understood in *Dhyâna*, or meditation. We hear a sound. First there is the external vibration, second, the nerve motion that carries it to the mind, third, the reaction from the mind, along with which flashes the knowledge of the object which was the external cause of these different changes from the ethereal vibrations to the mental reaction. These three are called in *Yoga*, *Śabdha* (sound) *Artha* (meaning), and *Jnâna* (knowledge). In the language of physiology they are called the ethereal vibration, the motion in the nerve and brain, and the mental reaction. Now these, though distinct processes, have become mixed up in such a fashion as to become quite indistinct. In fact, we cannot now perceive any of these causes; we only perceive the effect of these three, which effect we call the external object. Every act of perception includes these three, and there is no reason why we should not be able to distinguish between them.

When, by the previous preparations, the mind becomes strong and controlled, and the power of finer perception has been attained, then the mind should be employed in meditation. This meditation must begin with gross objects and slowly rise to finer, then to finer and finer, until it has become objectless. The mind should first be employed in perceiving the external causes of sensations, then the internal motions, and then the reaction of the mind. When it has succeeded in perceiving the external causes of sensations by themselves it will acquire the power of perceiving all fine material existences, all fine bodies and forms. When it can succeed in perceiving the motions inside, by themselves, it will gain the control of all mental waves, in itself or in others, even before they have translated themselves into physical forces; and when he will be able to perceive the mental reaction by itself the *Yogî* will acquire the knowledge of everything, as every sensible object, and every thought, is the result of this reaction. Then will he have seen, as it were, the very foundations of his mind, and it will be under his perfect control. Different powers will come to the *Yogî*, and if he yields to the temptations of any one of these the road to his further progress will be barred. Such is the evil of running after enjoyments. But, if he is strong enough to reject even these miraculous powers, he will attain to the goal of *Yoga*, the complete suppression of the waves in the ocean of the mind; then the glory of the soul, untrammelled by the distractions of the mind, or the motions of his body, will shine in its full effulgence. And the *Yogî* will find himself as he is and as he always was, the essence of knowledge, the immortal, the all-pervading.

Samâdhi is the property of every human being — nay, every animal. From the lowest animal to the highest angelic being, some time or other each one will have to come to that state, and then, and then alone, will religion begin for him. And all this time, what are we doing? We are only struggling towards that stage; there is now no difference between us and those who have no religion, because we have had no experience. What is concentration good for, save to bring us to this experience? Each one of the steps to attain this *Samâdhi* has been reasoned out, properly adjusted, scientifically organised, and, when faithfully practised, will surely lead us to the desired end. Then will all sorrows cease, all miseries vanish; the seeds of actions will be burned, and the soul will be free for ever.

CHAPTER VIII.

RÂJA YOGA IN BRIEF.

THIS is a summary of *Râja Yoga* freely translated from the *Kurma Purâna.*

The fire of *Yoga* burns the cage of sin that is around a man. Knowledge becomes purified, and *Nirvâna* is directly obtained. From *Yoga* comes knowledge; knowledge again helps the *Yogî*. He who is a compound of both *Yoga* and knowledge, with him the Lord is pleased. Those that practice *Mahâyoga*, either once a day, or twice a day, or thrice, or always, know them to be gods. *Yoga* is divided into two parts. One is called the *Abhâva*, and the other *Mahâyoga*. Where one's self is meditated upon as zero, and bereft of quality, that is called *Abhâva;* the *Yogî*, by each one, realises his Self. That in which one sees the Self as full of bliss and bereft of all impurities, and one with God, is called *Mahâyoga*. The other *Yogas* that we read and hear of, do not deserve one particle of this great *Brahmayoga*, in which the *Yogî* finds himself and the whole universe as God himself. This is the highest of all *Yogas*.

These are the steps in *Râja Yoga*. *Yama*, *Niyama*, *Âsana*, *Prâṇâyâma*, *Pratyâhâra*, *Dhâraṇâ*, *Dhyâna*, and *Samâdhi*, of which, non-injuring anybody, truthfulness, non-covetousness, chastity, not receiving anything from another, are called *Yama;* it purifies the mind, the *Chitta*. By thought, word, and deed, always, and in every living being, not producing pain is what is called *Ahimsa*, non-injuring. There is no virtue higher than this non-injuring. There is no happiness higher than what a man obtains by this attitude of non-offensiveness to all creation. By truth we attain to work. Through truth everything is attained; in truth everything is established. Relating facts as they are; this is truth. Not taking others' goods by stealth or by force, is called *Asteyam*, non-covetousness. Chastity in thought, word, and deed, always, and in all conditions, is what is called *Brahmacharya*. Not receiving any present from anybody, even when one is suffering terribly, is what is called *Aparigraha*. When a man receives a gift from another man, the theory is that his heart becomes impure, he becomes low, he loses his independence, he becomes bound and attached. The following are helps to success in *Yoga*. *Niyama*, regular habits and observances; *Tapas*, austerity; *Svâdhyâya*, study; *Santośa*, contentment; *Saucham*, purity; *Îśwara pranidhâna*, worshipping God. Fasting, or in other ways controlling the body, is called the physical *Tapas*.

Repeating the *Vedas*, and other *Mantrams*, by which the *Sattva* material in the body is purified, is called study, *Svâdhyâya*. There are three sorts of repetitions of these *Mantrams*. One is called the verbal, another semi-verbal, and the third mental. The verbal or audible is the lowest, and the inaudible is the highest of all. The repetition which is so loud that anybody can hear it is the verbal; the next one is where only the organs begin to vibrate, but no sound is heard; another man sitting near cannot hear what is being said. That in which there is no sound, only mental repetition of the *Mantram*, at the same time thinking of its meaning, is called the "mental muttering," and is the highest. The sages have said that there are two sorts of purification, external and internal. The purification for the body is by water, earth, or other materials; the external purification, as by bathing, etc. Purification of the mind by truth, and by all the other virtues, is what is called internal purification. Both are necessary. It is not sufficient that a man should be internally pure and externally dirty. When both are not attainable the internal purity is the better, but no one will be a *Yogî* until he has both.

Worship is by praise, by memory, having devotion to God. We have spoken about *Yama* and *Niyama*; next comes *Prâṇâyâma*. *Prâṇa* means the vital forces in one's own body, *Yama* means controlling them. There are three sorts of *Prâṇâyâma*, the very simple, the middle, and the very high. The whole of *Prâṇâyâma* is divided into two parts; one is called filling, and the other is called emptying. When you begin with twelve seconds it is the lowest *Prâṇâyâma*; when you begin with twenty-four seconds it is the middle *Prâṇâyâma*; that *Prâṇâyâma* is the best which begins with thirty-six seconds. That *Prâṇâyâma* in which there is first perspiration, then vibration of the body, and then rising from the seat and joining of the man's soul with great bliss is the very highest *Prâṇâyâma*. There is a *Mantram* called the *Gâyatri*. It is a very holy verse of the *Vedas*. "We meditate on the glory of that Being who has produced this universe; may He enlighten our minds." Then *Om* is joined to it, at the beginning and end. In one *Prâṇâyâma* repeat three *Gâyatris*. In all books they speak of *Prâṇâyâma* being divided into *Rechaka* (rejecting or exhaling), *Pûraka* (inhaling), and *Kumbhaka* (restraining, stationary). The *Indriyas*, the organs of the senses, are acting outwards and coming in contact with external objects. Bringing them under the control of the will is what is called *Pratyâhâra;* gathering towards oneself is the literal translation.

Fixing the mind on the lotus of the heart, or on the centre of the head, is what is called *Dhâraṇâ*. When remaining in one place, making one place as the base, when the waves of the mind rise up, without being touched by other waves — when all other waves have stopped — and one wave only rises in the mind, that is called *Dhyâna*, meditation. When no basis is necessary, when the whole of the mind has become one wave, "one-formedness," it is called *Samâdhi*. Bereft of all help from places and centres, only the meaning of the thing is present. If the mind can be fixed on one centre for twelve seconds it will be a *Dhâraṇâ*, twelve such *Dhâraṇâs* will be a *Dhyâna*, and twelve such *Dhyânas* will be a *Samâdhi*. The next is *Âsana* (posture). The only thing to understand is to hold the body straight, leaving the body free, with the chest, shoulders, and head straight. Where there is fire, or in water, or on ground which is strewn with dry leaves, or where there are wild animals, where four streets meet, or where there is too much noise, or too much fear, or too many ant hills, where there are many wicked persons, *Yoga* must not be practiced in such places. This applies more particularly to India. When the body feels very lazy do not practise, or when the mind is very miserable and sorrowful, or when the body is ill. Go to a place which is well hidden, and where people do not come to disturb you. As soon as you do not want people to know what you are doing all the curiosity in the world will be awakened, but, if you go into the street and want people to know what you are doing, they will not care. Do not choose dirty places. Rather choose beautiful scenery, or a room in your own house which is beautiful. When you practise, first salute all the ancient *Yogîs*, and your own *Gurû*, and God, and then begin.

Dhyâna is spoken of, and a few examples are given of what to meditate upon. Sit straight, and look at the tip of your nose. Later on we will come to know how that concentrates the mind, how by controlling the two optic nerves one advances a long way towards the control of the arc of reaction, and so to the control of the will. These are a few specimens of meditation. Imagine a lotus upon the top of the head, several inches up, and virtue as its centre, the stalk as knowledge. The eight petals of the lotus are the eight powers of the *Yogî*. Inside, the stamens and pistils are renunciation. If the *Yogî* refuses the external powers he will come to salvation. So the eight petals of the lotus are the eight powers, but the internal stamens and pistils are the extreme renunciation, the renunciation of all these. Inside of that lotus think of the Golden One, the Almighty, the Intangible, He whose name is *Om*, the Inexpressible, surrounded with effulgent light. Meditate on that. Another meditation is given. Think of a space in your heart, and in the midst of that space think that a flame is burning. Think of that flame as your own soul, and inside that flame is another space, effulgent, and that is the Soul of your soul, God. Meditate upon that in the heart. Chastity, non-injuring, pardoning everyone, even the greatest enemy, truth, faith in the Lord, these are all different *Vṛittis*. Be not afraid if you are not perfect in all of these; work, and the others will come. He who has given up all attachment, all fear, and all anger, he whose whole soul has gone unto the Lord, he who has taken refuge in the Lord, whose heart has become purified, with whatsoever desire he comes to the Lord He will grant that to him. Therefore worship Him through knowledge, or worship Him through love, or worship Him through renunciation.

"He is my beloved worshipper, he is my beloved *Bhakta*, who is not jealous of any being, who is the friend of all, who is merciful to all, who has nothing of his own, whose egotism is lost; he who is always satisfied; he who works always in *Yoga*, whose self has become controlled, whose will is firm, whose mind and whose intelligence are given up unto me, know that he is my beloved *Bhakta*. From whom comes no disturbance, who never becomes the cause of disturbance to others, he who has given up excessive joy, grief, and fear, and anxiety. Such a one is my beloved. He who does not depend on anything, pure, active, giving up all, who does not care whether good comes or evil, never becomes miserable; he who is the same in praise or in blame, with a silent, thoughtful mind, blessed with what little comes in his way, homeless, he who has no home, the whole world is his home, steady in his ideas, such a one becomes a *Yogî*."

There was a great god-sage called *Nârada*. Just as there are sages among mankind, great *Yogîs*, so there are great *Yogîs* among the gods. *Nârada* was a good *Yogî*, and very great. He travelled everywhere, and one day he was passing through a forest, and he saw a man who had been meditating until the white ants had built a huge mound round his body, he had been sitting in that position so long. He said to *Nârada*, "Where are you going?" *Nârada* replied, "I am going to heaven." "Then ask God when He will be merciful to me; when I will attain freedom." Further on *Nârada* saw another man. He was jumping about, singing, dancing, and said, "Oh, *Nârada*, where are you going?" His voice and his gestures were wild. *Nârada* said, "I am going to heaven." "Then, ask when I will be free." So *Nârada* went on. In the course of time he came again by the same road, and there was the man who had been meditating till the ant-hills had grown round him. He said, "Oh, *Nârada*, did you ask the Lord about me?" "Oh, yes." "What did He say?" "The Lord told me that you would attain freedom in four more births." Then the man began to weep and wail, and said, "I have meditated until an ant-hill has been raised around me, and I have four more births yet!" *Nârada* went to the other man. "Did you ask my question?" "Oh, yes. Do you see this tamarind tree? I have to tell you that as many leaves as there are on that tree, so many times you will be born, and then you will attain freedom." Then the man began to dance for joy, and said, "I will have freedom after such a short time." A voice came, "My child, you will have freedom this minute." That was the reward for his perseverance. He was ready to work through all those births, nothing discouraged him. But the first man felt that even four more births must be too long. Only perseverance like that of the man who was willing to wait æons will bring about the highest result.

PATANJALI'S

YOGA APHORISMS

PATANJALI'S

YOGA APHORISMS

INTRODUCTION.

BEFORE going into the *Yoga* Aphorisms I will try to discuss one great question, upon which the whole theory of religion rests, for the *Yogîs*. It seems the consensus of opinion of the great minds of the world, and it has been nearly demonstrated by researches into physical nature, that we are the outcome and manifestation of an absolute condition, back of our present relative condition, and are going forward, to return again to that absolute. This being granted, the question is, which is better, the absolute or this state? There are not wanting people who think that this manifested state is the highest state of man. Thinkers of great calibre are of the opinion that we are manifested specimens of undifferentiated being, and this differentiated state is higher than the absolute. Because in the absolute there cannot be any quality they imagine that it must be insensate, dull, and lifeless, that only this life can be enjoyed, and therefore we must cling to it. First of all we want to inquire into other solutions of life. There was an old solution that man after death remained the same, that all his good sides, minus his evil sides, remained for ever. Logically stated this means that man's goal is the world; this world carried a stage higher, and with elimination of its evils is the state they call heaven. This theory, on the face of it, is absurd and puerile, because it cannot be. There cannot be good without evil, or evil without good. To live in a world where it is all good and no evil is what Sanskrit logicians call a "dream in the air." Another theory in modern times has been presented by several schools, that man's destiny is to go on always improving, always struggling towards, and never reaching, the goal. This statement, though, apparently, very nice, is also absurd, because there is no such thing as motion in a straight line. Every motion is in a circle. If you could take up a stone, and project it into space, and then live long enough, that stone would come back exactly to your hand. A straight line, infinitely projected, must end in a circle. Therefore, this idea that the destiny of man is progression ever forward and forward, and never stopping, is absurd. Although extraneous to the subject, I may remark that this idea explains the ethical theory that you must not hate, and must love, because, just as in the case of electricity, or any other force, the modern theory is that the power leaves the dynamo and completes the circle back to the dynamo. So with all forces in nature; they must come back to the source. Therefore do not hate anybody, because that force, that hatred, which comes out from you, must, in the long run, come back to you. If you love, that love will come back to you, completing the circuit. It is as certain as can be, that every bit of hatred that goes out of the heart of man comes back to him in full force; nothing can stop it, and every impulse of love comes back to him. On other and practical grounds we see that the theory of eternal progression is untenable, for destruction is the goal of everything earthly. All our struggles and hopes and fears and joys, what will they lead to? We will all end in death. Nothing is so certain as this. Where, then, is this motion in a straight line? This infinite progression? It is only going out to a distance, and again coming back to the centre from which it started. See how, from nebulæ, the sun, moon, and stars, are produced; then they dissolve, and go back to nebulæ. The same is being done everywhere. The plant takes material from the earth, dissolves, and gives it back. Every form in this world is taken out of surrounding atoms and goes back to these atoms.

It cannot be that the same law acts differently in different places. Law is uniform. Nothing is more certain than that. If this is the law of nature, so it is with thought; it will dissolve and come back to its origin; whether we will it or not we shall have to return to the origin, which is called God or Absolute. We all came from God, and we are all bound to go to God, call that God by any name you like; call Him God, or Absolute or Nature, or by any hundred names you like, the fact remains the same. "From whom all this universe comes out, in whom all that is born lives, and to whom all returns." This is one fact that is certain. Nature works on the same plan; what is being worked out in one sphere is being worked out in millions of spheres. What you see with the planets, the same will it be with this earth, with men and with the stars. The huge wave is a mighty compound of small waves, it may be of millions; the life of the whole world is a compound of millions of little lives, and the death of the whole world is the compound of the deaths of these millions of little beings.

Now the question arises, is going back to God the higher state, or is it not? The philosophers of the *Yoga* school emphatically answer that it is. They say that man's present state is a degeneration; there is no one religion on the face of the earth which says that man is an improvement. The idea is that his beginning is perfect and pure, that he degenerates until he cannot degenerate further, and that there must come a time when he shoots upward again to complete the circle; the circle must be there. However low he goes, he must ultimately take the upward bend again, and go back to the original source, which is God. Man comes from God in the beginning, in the middle he becomes man, and in the end he goes back to God. This is the method of putting it in the Dualistic form. In the Monistic form you say that man is God, and goes back to Him again. If our present state is the higher one, then why is there so much horror and misery, and why is there an end to it? If this is the higher state, why does it end? That which corrupts and degenerates cannot be the highest state. Why should it be so diabolical, so unsatisfying? It is only excusable, inasmuch as, through it, we are taking a higher groove; we have to pass through it in order to become regenerate again. Put a seed into the ground and it disintegrates, dissolves after a time, and out of that dissolution comes the splendid tree. Every seed must degenerate to become the stately tree. So it follows that the sooner we get out of this state we call "man" the better for us. Is it by committing suicide that we get out of this state? Not at all. That will be making it all the worse. Torturing ourselves, or condemning the world, is not the way to get out. We have to pass through the "Slough of Despond," and the sooner we are through the better. But it must always be remembered that this is not the highest state.

The really difficult part to understand is that this state, the Absolute, which has been called the highest, is not, as some fear, that of the zoophite, or of the stone. That would be a dangerous thing to think. According to these thinkers there are only two states of existence, one of the stone, and the other of thought. What right have they to limit existence to these two? Is there not something infinitely superior to thought? The vibrations of light, when they are very low, we do not see; when they become a little more intense they become light to us; when they become still more intense we do not see them; it is dark to us. Is the darkness in the end the same as in the beginning?

Certainly not; it is the difference of the two poles. Is the thoughtlessness of the stone the same as the thoughtlessness of God? Certainly not. God does not think; He does not reason; why should He? Is anything unknown to Him, that He should reason? The stone cannot reason; God does not. Such is the difference. These philosophers think it is awful if we go beyond thought; they find nothing beyond thought.

There are much higher states of existence beyond reasoning. It is really beyond the intellect that the first state of religious life is to be found. When you step beyond thought and intellect and all reasoning, then you have made the first step towards God; and that is the beginning of life. This that is commonly called life is but an embryo state.

The next question will be, what proof is there that this state beyond thought and reasoning is the highest state? In the first place, all the great men of the world, much greater than those that only talk, men who moved the world, men who never thought of any selfish ends whatever, have declared that this is but a little stage on the way, that the Infinite is beyond. In the second place, they not only say so, but lay it open to everyone, they leave their methods, and all can follow in their steps. In the third place, there is no other way left. There is no other explanation. Taking for granted that there is no higher state, why are we going through this circle all the time; what reason can explain the world? The sensible will be the limit to our knowledge if we cannot go farther, if we must not ask for anything more. This is what is called agnosticism. But what reason is there to believe in the testimony of the senses? I would call that man a true agnostic who would stand still in the street and die. If reason is all in all it leaves us no place to stand on this side of nihilism. If a man is agnostic of everything but money, fame and name, he is only a fraud. Kant has proved beyond all doubt that we cannot penetrate beyond the tremendous dead wall called reason. But that is the very first idea upon which all Indian thought takes its stand, and dares to seek, and succeeds in finding something higher than reason, where alone the explanation of the present state is to be found. This is the value of the study of something that will take us beyond the world. "Thou art our Father, and wilt take us to the other shore of this ocean of ignorance;" that is the science of religion; nothing else can be.

THE YOGA APHORISMS

CHAPTER I.

1. Now concentration is explained.

2. Yoga is restraining the mind-stuff (Chitta) from taking various forms (Vṛittis).

A good deal of explanation is necessary here. We have to understand what *Chitta* is, and what are these *Vṛittis*. I have this eye. Eyes do not see. Take away the brain centre which is in the head, the eyes will still be there, the retinæ complete, and also the picture, and yet the eyes will not see. So the eyes are only a secondary instrument, not the organ of vision. The organ of vision is in the nerve centre of the brain. The two eyes will not be sufficient alone. Sometimes a man is asleep with his eyes open. The light is there and the picture is there, but a third thing is necessary; mind must be joined to the organ. The eye is the external instrument, we need also the brain centre and the agency of the mind. Carriages roll down a street and you do not hear them. Why? Because your mind has not attached itself to the organ of hearing. First, there is the instrument, then there is the organ, and third, the mind attachment to these two. The mind takes the impression farther in, and presents it to the determinative faculty—*Buddhi*—which reacts. Along with this reaction flashes the idea of egoism. Then this mixture of action and reaction is presented to the *Puruṣa*, the real Soul, who perceives an object in this mixture. The organs (*Indriyas*), together with the mind (*Manas*), the determinative faculty (*Buddhi*), and egoism (*Ahamkâra*), form the group called the *Antahkaraṇa* (the internal instrument). They are but various processes in the mind-stuff, called *Chitta*. The waves of thought in the *Chitta* are called *Vṛitti* ("the whirlpool" is the literal translation). What is thought? Thought is a force, as is gravitation or repulsion. It is absorbed from the infinite storehouse of force in nature; the instrument called *Chitta* takes hold of that force, and, when it passes out at the other end it is called thought. This force is supplied to us through food, and out of that food the body obtains the power of motion, etc. Others, the finer forces, it throws out in what we call thought. Naturally we see that the mind is not intelligent; yet it appears to be intelligent. Why? Because the intelligent soul is behind it. You are the only sentient being; mind is only the instrument through which you catch the external world. Take this book; as a book it does not exist outside, what exists outside is unknown and unknowable. It is the suggestion that gives a blow to the mind, and the mind gives out the reaction. If a stone is thrown into the water the water is thrown against it in the form of waves. The real universe is the occasion of the reaction of the mind. A book form, or an elephant form, or a man form, is not outside; all that we know is our mental reaction from the outer suggestion. Matter is the "permanent possibility of sensation," said John Stuart Mill. It is only the suggestion that is outside. Take an oyster for example. You know how pearls are made. A grain of sand or something gets inside and begins to irritate it, and the oyster throws a sort of enamelling around the sand, and this makes the pearl. This whole universe is our own enamel, so to say, and the real universe is the grain of sand. The ordinary man will never understand it, because, when he tries to, he throws out an enamel, and sees only his own enamel. Now we understand what is meant by these *Vṛittis*. The real man is behind the mind, and the mind is the instrument in his hands, and it is his intelligence that is percolating through it. It is only when you stand behind it that it becomes intelligent. When man gives it up it falls to pieces, and is nothing. So you understand what is meant by *Chitta*. It is the mind-stuff, and *Vṛittis* are the waves and ripples rising in it when external causes impinge on it. These *Vṛittis* are our whole universe.

The bottom of the lake we cannot see, because its surface is covered with ripples. It is only possible when the ripples have subsided, and the water is calm, for us to catch a glimpse of the bottom. If the water is muddy, the bottom will not be seen; if the water is agitated all the time, the bottom will not be seen. If the water is clear, and there are no waves, we shall see the bottom. That bottom of the lake is our own true Self; the lake is the *Chitta*, and the waves the *Vṛittis*. Again, this mind is in three states; one is darkness, which is called *Tamas*, just as in brutes and idiots; it only acts to injure others. No other idea comes into that state of mind. Then there is the active state of mind, *Rajas*, whose chief motives are power and enjoyment. "I will be powerful and rule others." Then, at last, when the waves cease, and the water of the lake becomes clear, there is the state called *Sattva*, serenity, calmness. It is not inactive, but rather intensely active. It is the greatest manifestation of power to be calm. It is easy to be active. Let the reins go, and the horses will drag you down. Any one can do that, but he who can stop the plunging horses is the strong man. Which requires the greater strength, letting go, or restraining? The calm man is not the man who is dull. You must not mistake *Sattva* for dulness, or laziness. The calm man is the one who has restraint of these waves. Activity is the manifestation of the lower strength, calmness of the superior strength.

This *Chitta* is always trying to get back to its natural pure state, but the organs draw it out. To restrain it, and to check this outward tendency, and to start it on the return journey to that essence of intelligence is the first step in *Yoga*, because only in this way can the *Chitta* get into its proper course.

Although this *Chitta* is in every animal, from the lowest to the highest, it is only in the human form that we find intellect, and until the mind-stuff can take the form of intellect it is not possible for it to return through all these steps, and liberate the soul. Immediate salvation is impossible for the cow and the dog, although they have mind, because their *Chitta* cannot as yet take that form which we call intellect.

Chitta manifests itself in all these different forms — scattering, darkening, weakening, and concentrating. These are the four states in which the mind-stuff manifests itself. First a scattered form, is activity. Its tendency is to manifest in the form of pleasure or of pain. Then the dull form is darkness, the only tendency of which is to injure others. The commentator says the first form is natural to the *Devas*, the angels, and the second is the demoniacal form. *Vikshipta* is when it struggles to centre itself. The *Ekâgra*, the concentrated form of the *Chitta*, is what brings us to *Samâdhi*.

3. At that time (the time of concentration) the seer (the Puruṣa) rests in his own (unmodified) state.

As soon as the waves have stopped, and the lake has become quiet, we see the ground below the lake. So with the mind; when it is calm, we see what our own nature is; we do not mix ourselves but remain our own selves.

4. At other times (other than that of concentration) the seer is identified with the modifications.

For instance, I am in a state of sorrow; some one blames me; this is a modification, *Vṛitti*, and I identify myself with it, and the result is misery.

5. There are five classes of modifications, painful and not painful.

6. (These are) right knowledge, indiscrimination, verbal delusion, sleep, and memory.

7. Direct perception, inference, and competent evidence, are proofs.

When two of our perceptions do not contradict each other we call it proof. I hear something, and, if it contradicts something already perceived, I begin to fight it out, and do not believe it. There are also three kinds of proof. Direct perception, *Pratyaksham*, whatever we see and feel, is proof, if there has been nothing to delude the senses. I see the world; that is sufficient proof that it exists. Secondly, *Anumâna*, inference; you see a sign, and from the sign you come to the thing signified. Thirdly, *Âptavâkyam*, the direct perception of the *Yogî*, of those who have seen the truth. We are all of us struggling towards knowledge, but you and I have to struggle hard, and come to knowledge through a long tedious process of reasoning, but the *Yogî*, the pure one, has gone beyond all this. Before his mind, the past, the present, and the future, are alike one book for him to read; he does not require to go through all this tedious process, and his words are proofs, because he sees knowledge in himself; he is the Omniscient One. These, for instance, are the authors of the Sacred Scriptures; therefore the Scriptures are proof, and, if any such persons are living now, their words will be proof. Other philosophers go into long discussions about this *Âpta*, and they say, what is the proof that this is truth? The proof is because they see it; because whatever I see is proof, and whatever you see is proof, if it does not contradict any past knowledge. There is knowledge beyond the senses, and whenever it does not contradict reason and past human experience, that knowledge is proof. Any madman may come into this room and say he sees angels around him; that would not be proof. In the first place it must be true knowledge, and, secondly, it must not contradict knowledge of the past, and, thirdly, it must depend upon the character of the man. I hear it said that the character of the man is not of so much importance as what he may say; we must first hear what he says. This may be true in other things; a man may be wicked, and yet make an astronomical discovery, but in religion it is different, because no impure man will ever have the power to reach the truths of religion. Therefore, we have first of all to see that the man who declares himself to be an *Âpta* is a perfectly unselfish and holy person; secondly that he has reached beyond the senses, and thirdly that what he says does not contradict the past knowledge of humanity. Any new discovery of truth does not contradict the past truth, but fits into it. And, fourthly, that truth must have a possibility of verification. If a man says "I have seen a vision," and tells me that I have no right to see it, I believe him not. Every one must have the power to see it for himself. No one who sells his knowledge is an *Âpta*. All these conditions must be fulfilled; you must first see that the man is pure, and that he has no selfish motive; that he has no thirst for gain or fame. Secondly, he must show that he is super-conscious. Thirdly, he must give us something that we cannot get from our senses, and which is for the benefit of the world. And we must see that it does not contradict other truths; if it contradict other scientific truths reject it at once. Fourthly, the man should never be singular; he should only represent what all men can attain. The three sorts of proof, are, then, direct sense perception, inference, and the words of an *Âpta*. I cannot translate this word into English. It is not the word inspired, because that comes from outside, while this comes from himself. The literal meaning is "attained."

8. Indiscrimination is false knowledge not established in real nature.

The next class of *Vṛittis* that arise is mistaking the one thing for another, as a piece of mother-of-pearl is taken for a piece of silver.

9. Verbal delusion follows from words having no (corresponding) reality.

There is another class of *Vṛittis* called *Vikalpa.* A word is uttered, and we do not wait to consider its meaning; we jump to a conclusion immediately. It is the sign of weakness of the *Chitta.* Now you can understand the theory of restraint. The weaker the man the less he has of restraint. Consider yourselves always in that way. When you are going to be angry or miserable, reason it out, how it is that some news that has come to you is throwing your mind into *Vṛittis.*

10. Sleep is a Vritti which embraces the feeling of voidness.

The next class of *Vṛittis* is called sleep and dream. When we awake we know that we have been sleeping; we can only have memory of perception. That which we do not perceive we never can have any memory of. Every reaction is a wave in the lake. Now, if, during sleep, the mind had no waves, it would have no perceptions, positive or negative, and, therefore, we would not remember them. The very reason of our remembering sleep is that during sleep there was a certain class of waves in the mind. Memory is another class of *Vṛittis,* which is called *Smṛiti.*

11. Memory is when the (Vṛittis of) perceived subjects do not slip away (and through impressions come back to consciousness).

Memory can be caused by the previous three. For instance, you hear a word. That word is like a stone thrown into the lake of the *Chitta;* it causes a ripple, and that ripple rouses a series of ripples; this is memory. So in sleep. When the peculiar kind of ripple called sleep throws the *Chitta* into a ripple of memory it is called a dream. Dream is another form of the ripple which in the waking state is called memory.

12. Their control is by practice and non-attachment.

The mind, to have this non-attachment, must be clear, good and rational. Why should we practise? Because each action is like the pulsations quivering over the surface of the lake. The vibration dies out, and what is left? The *Samskâras*, the impressions. When a large number of these impressions is left on the mind they coalesce, and become a habit. It is said "habit is second nature;" it is first nature also, and the whole nature of man; everything that we are is the result of habit. That gives us consolation, because, if it is only habit, we can make and unmake it at any time. This *Samskâra* is left by these vibrations passing out of our mind, each one of them leaving its result Our character is the sum-total of these marks, and according as some particular wave prevails one takes that tone. If good prevail one becomes good, if wickedness one becomes wicked, if joyfulness one becomes happy. The only remedy for bad habits is counter habits; all the bad habits that have left their impressions are to be controlled by good habits. Go on doing good, thinking holy thoughts continuously; that is the only way to suppress base impressions. Never say any man is hopeless, because he only represents a character, a bundle of habits, and these can be checked by new and better ones. Character is repeated habits, and repeated habits alone can reform character.

13. Continuous struggle to keep them (the Vṛittis) perfectly restrained is practice.

What is this practice? The attempt to restrain the mind in the *Chitta* form, to prevent its going out into waves.

14. Its ground becomes firm by long, constant efforts with great love (for the end to be attained).

Restraint does not come in one day, but by long continued practice.

15. That effect which comes to those who have given up their thirst after objects either seen or heard, and which wills to control the objects, is non-attachment.

Two motives of our actions are (1) What we see ourselves; (2) The experience of others. These two forces are throwing the mind, the lake, into various waves. Renunciation is the power of battling against these, and holding the mind in check. Renunciation of these two motives is what we want. I am passing through a street, and a man comes and takes my watch. That is my own experience. I see it myself, and it immediately throws my *Chitta* into a wave, taking the form of anger. Allow not that to come. If you cannot prevent that, you are nothing; if you can, you have *Vairâgyam.* Similarly, the experience of the worldly-minded teaches us that sense enjoyments are the highest ideal. These are tremendous temptations. To deny them, and not allow the mind to come into a wave form with regard to them, is renunciation; to control the twofold motive powers arising from my own experience, and from the experience of others, and thus prevent the *Chitta* from being governed by them, is *Vairâgyam.* These should be controlled by me, and not I by them. This sort of mental strength is called renunciation. This *Vairâgyam* is the only way to freedom.

16. That extreme non-attachment, giving up even the qualities, shows (the real nature of) the Puruṣa.

It is the highest manifestation of power when it takes away even our attraction towards the qualities. We have first to understand what the *Puruṣa*, the Self, is, and what are the qualities. According to *Yoga* philosophy the whole of nature consists of three qualities; one is called *Tamas*, another *Rajas*, and the third *Sattva*. These three qualities manifest themselves in the physical world as attraction, repulsion, and control. Everything that is in nature, all these manifestations, are combinations and recombinations of these three forces. This nature has been divided into various categories by the *Sânkhyas;* the Self of man is beyond all these, beyond nature, is effulgent by Its very nature. It is pure and perfect. Whatever of intelligence we see in nature is but the reflection from this Self upon nature. Nature itself is insentient. You must remember that the word nature also includes the mind; mind is in nature; thought is in nature; from thought, down to the grossest form of matter, everything is in nature, the manifestation of nature. This nature has covered the Self of man, and when nature takes away the covering the Self becomes unveiled, and appears in Its own glory. This non-attachment, as it is described in Aphorism 15 (as being control of nature) is the greatest help towards manifesting the Self. The next aphorism defines *Samâdhi*, perfect concentration, which is the goal of the *Yogî*.

17. The concentration called right knowledge is that which is followed by reasoning, discrimination, bliss, unqualified ego.

This *Samâdhi* is divided into two varieties. One is called the *Samprajnâta*, and the other the *Asamprajnâta*. The *Samprajnâta* is of four varieties. In this *Samâdhi* come all the powers of controlling nature. The first variety is called the *Savitarka*, when the mind meditates upon an object again and again, by isolating it from other objects. There are two sorts of objects for meditation, the categories of nature, and the *Puruṣa*. Again, the categories are of two varieties; the twenty-four categories are insentient, and the one sentient is the *Puruṣa*. When the mind thinks of the elements of nature by thinking of their beginning and their end, this is one sort of *Savitarka*. The words require explanation. This part of *Yoga* is based entirely on *Sânkhya* Philosophy, about which I have already told you. As you will remember, egoism and will, and mind, have a common basis, and that common basis is called the *Chitta*, the mind-stuff, out of which they are all manufactured. This mind-stuff takes in the forces of nature, and projects them as thought. There must be something, again, where both force and matter are one. This is called *Avyaktam*, the unmanifested state of nature, before creation, and to which, after the end of a cycle, the whole of nature returns, to again come out after another period. Beyond that is the *Puruṣa*, the essence of intelligence. There is no liberation in getting powers. It is a worldly search after enjoyments, and there is no enjoyment in this life; all search for enjoyment is vain; this is the old, old lesson which man finds it so hard to learn. When he does learn it, he gets out of the universe and becomes free. The possession of what are called occult powers is only intensifying the world, and in the end, intensifying suffering. Though, as a scientist, *Patanjali* is bound to point out the possibilities of this science, he never misses an opportunity to warn us against these powers. Knowledge is power, and as soon as we begin to know a thing we get power over it; so also, when the mind begins to meditate on the different elements it gains power over them. That sort of meditation where the external gross elements are the objects is called *Savitarka*. *Tarka* means question, *Savitarka* with-question. Questioning the elements, as it were, that they may give up their truths and their powers to the man who meditates upon them. Again, in the very same meditation, when one struggles to take the elements out of time and space, and think of them as they are, it is called *Nirvitarka*, without-question. When the meditation goes a step higher, and takes the *Tanmâtras* as its object, and thinks of them as in time and space, it is called *Savichâra*, with-discrimination, and when the same meditation gets beyond time and space, and thinks of the fine elements as they are, it is called *Nirvichâra*, without-discrimination. The next step is when the elements are given up, either as gross or as fine, and the object of meditation is the interior organ, the thinking organ, and when the thinking organ is thought of as bereft of the qualities of activity, and of dulness, it is then called *Sânandam*, the blissful *Samâdhi*. In that *Samâdhi*, when we are thinking of the mind as the object of meditation, before we have reached the state which takes us beyond the mind even, when it has become very ripe and concentrated, when all ideas of the gross materials, or fine materials, have been given up, and the only object is the mind as it is, when the *Sattva* state only of the *Ego* remains, but differentiated from all other objects, this is called *Asmitâ Samâdhi*, and the man who has attained to this has attained to what is called in the *Vedas* "bereft of body." He can think of himself as without his gross body; but he will have to think of himself as with a fine body. Those that in this state get merged in nature without attaining the goal are called *Prakṛitilayas*, but those who do not even stop at any enjoyments, reach the goal, which is freedom.

18. There is another Samâdhi which is attained by the constant practice of cessation of all mental activity, in which the Chitta retains only the unmanifested impressions.

This is the perfect super-conscious *Asamprajnâta Samâdhi*, the state which gives us freedom. The first state does not give us freedom, does not liberate the soul. A man may attain to all powers, and yet fall again. There is no safeguard until the soul goes beyond nature, and beyond conscious concentration. It is very difficult to attain, although its method seems very easy. Its method is to hold the mind as the object, and whenever thought comes, to strike it down, allowing no thought to come into the mind, thus making it an entire vacuum. When we can really do this, in that moment we shall attain liberation. When persons without training and preparation try to make their minds vacant they are likely to succeed only in covering themselves with *Tamas*, material of ignorance, which makes the mind dull and stupid, and leads them to think that they are making a vacuum of the mind. To be able to really do that is a manifestation of the greatest strength, of the highest control. When this state, *Asamprajnâta*, super-consciousness, is reached, the *Samâdhi* becomes seedless. What is meant by that? In that sort of concentration when there is consciousness, where the mind has succeeded only in quelling the waves in the *Chitta* and holding them down, they are still there in the form of tendencies, and these tendencies (or seeds) will become waves again, when the time comes. But when you have destroyed all these tendencies, almost destroyed the mind, then it has become seedless, there are no more seeds in the mind out of which to manufacture again and again this plant of life, this ceaseless round of birth and death. You may ask, what state would that be, in which we should have no knowledge? What we call knowledge is a lower state than the one beyond knowledge. You must always bear in mind that the extremes look very much the same. The low vibration of light is darkness, and the very high vibration of light is darkness also, but one is real darkness, and the other is really intense light; yet their appearance is the same. So, ignorance is the lowest state, knowledge is the middle state, and beyond knowledge is a still higher state. Knowledge itself is a manufactured something, a combination; it is not reality. What will be the result of constant practice of this higher concentration? All old tendencies of restlessness, and dulness, will be destroyed, as well as the tendencies of goodness too. It is just the same as with the metals that are used with gold to take off the dirt and alloy. When the ore is smelted down, the dross is burnt along with the alloy. So this constant controlling power will stop the previous bad tendencies, and, eventually, the good ones also. Those good and evil tendencies will suppress each other, and there will remain the Soul, in all its glorious splendour, untrammelled by either good or bad, and that Soul is omnipresent, omnipotent, and omniscient. By giving up all powers it has become omnipotent, by giving up all life it is beyond mortality; it has become life itself. Then the Soul will know It neither had birth nor death, neither want of heaven nor of earth. It will know that It neither came nor went; it was nature which was moving, and that movement was reflected upon the Soul. The form of the light is moving, it is reflected and cast by the camera upon the wall, and the wall foolishly thinks it is moving. So with all of us; it is the *Chitta* constantly moving, manipulating itself into various forms, and we think that we are these various forms. All these delusions will vanish. When that free Soul will command — not pray or beg, but command — then whatever It desires will be immediately fulfilled; whatever It wants It will be able to do. According to the *Sânkhya* Philosophy there is no God. It says that there cannot be any God of this universe, because if there were He must be a Soul, and a Soul must be one of two things, either bound or free. How can the soul that is bound by nature, or controlled by nature, create? It is itself a slave. On the other hand, what business has the soul that is free to create and manipulate all these things? It has no desires, so cannot have any need to create. Secondly, it says the theory of God is an unnecessary one; nature explains all. What is the use of any God? But *Kapila* teaches that there are many souls, who, though nearly attaining perfection, fall short because they cannot perfectly renounce all powers. Their minds for a time merge in nature, to re-emerge as its masters. Such gods there are. We shall all become such gods, and, according to the *Sânkhyas*, the God spoken of in the *Vedas* really means one of these free souls. Beyond them there is not an eternally free and blessed Creator of the universe. On the other hand the *Yogîs* say, "Not so, there is a God; there is one Soul separate from all other souls, and He is the eternal Master of all creation, the Ever Free, the Teacher of all teachers." The *Yogîs* admit that those the *Sânkhyas* call the "merged in nature" also exist. They are *Yogîs* who have fallen short of perfection, and though, for a time debarred from attaining the goal, remain as rulers of parts of the universe.

19. (This Samâdhi, when not followed by extreme non-attachment) becomes the cause of the re-manifestation of the gods and of those that become merged in nature.

The gods in the Indian systems represent certain high offices which are being filled successively by various souls. But none of them is perfect.

20. To others (this Samâdhi) comes through faith, energy, memory, concentration, and discrimination of the real.

These are they who do not want the position of gods, or even that of rulers of cycles. They attain to liberation.

21. Success is speedy for the extremely energetic.

22. They again differ according as the means are mild, medium or supreme.

23. Or by devotion to Iśvara.

24. Iśvara (the Supreme Ruler) is a special Puruṣa, untouched by misery, the results of actions, or desires.

We must again remember that this *Patanjali Yoga* Philosophy is based upon that of the *Sânkhyas*, only that in the latter there is no place for God, while with the *Yogîs* God has a place. The *Yogîs*, however, avoid many ideas about God, such as creating. God as the Creator of the Universe is not meant by the *Iśvara* of the *Yogîs*, although, according to the *Vedas*, *Iśvara* is the Creator of the universe. Seeing that the universe is harmonious, it must be the manifestation of one will. The *Yogîs* and *Sânkhyas* both avoid the question of creation. The *Yogîs* want to establish a God, but carefully avoid this question, they do not raise it at all. Yet you will find that they arrive at God in a peculiar fashion of their own. They say:

25. In Him becomes infinite that all-knowingness which in others is (only) a germ.

The mind must always travel between two extremes. You can think of limited space, but the very idea of that gives you also unlimited space. Close your eyes and think of a little space, and at the same time that you perceive the little circle, you have a circle round it of unlimited dimensions. It is the same with time. Try to think of a second, you will have, with the same act of perception, to think of time which is unlimited. So with knowledge. Knowledge is only a germ in man, but you will have to think of infinite knowledge around it, so that the very nature of your constitution shows us that there is unlimited knowledge, and the *Yogîs* call that unlimited knowledge God.

26. He is the Teacher of even the ancient teachers, being not limited by time.

It is true that all knowledge is within ourselves, but this has to be called forth by another knowledge. Although the capacity to know is inside us, it must be called out, and that calling out of knowledge can only be got, a *Yogî* maintains, through another knowledge. Dead, insentient matter, never calls out knowledge, it is the action of knowledge that brings our knowledge. Knowing beings must be with us to call forth what is in us, so these teachers were always necessary. The world was never without them, and no knowledge can come without them. God is the Teacher of all teachers, because these teachers, however great they may have been — gods or angels — were all bound and limited by time, and God is not limited by time. These are the two peculiar deductions of the *Yogîs*. The first is that in thinking of the limited, the mind must think of the unlimited, and that if one part of that perception is true the other must be, for the reason that their value as perceptions of the mind is equal. The very fact that man has a little knowledge, shows that God has unlimited knowledge. If I am to take one, why not the other? Reason forces me to take both or reject both. If I believe that there is a man with a little knowledge, I must also admit that there is someone behind him with unlimited knowledge. The second deduction is that no knowledge can come without a teacher. It is true as the modern philosophers say, that there is something in man which evolves out of him; all knowledge is in man, but certain environments are necessary to call it out. We cannot find any knowledge without teachers, if there are men teachers, god teachers, or angel teachers, they are all limited; who was the teacher before them? We are forced to admit, as a last conclusion, One Teacher, Who is not limited by time, and that One Teacher of infinite knowledge, without beginning or end, is called God.

27. His manifesting word is Om.

Every idea that you have in the mind has a counterpart in a word; the word and the thought are inseparable. The external part of the thought is what we call word, and the internal part is what we call thought. No man can, by analysis, separate thought from word. The idea that language was created by men — certain men sitting together and deciding upon words, has been proved to be wrong. So long as things have existed there have been words and language. What is the connection between an idea and a word? Although we see that there must always be a word with a thought, it is not necessary that the same thought requires the same word. The thought may be the same in twenty different countries, yet the language is different. We must have a word to express each thought, but these words need not necessarily have the same sound. Sounds will vary in different nations. Our commentator says "Although the relation between thought and word is perfectly natural, yet it does not mean a rigid connection between one sound and one idea." These sounds vary, yet the relation between the sounds and the thoughts is a natural one. The connection between thoughts and sounds is good only if there be a real connection between the thing signified and the symbol, and until then that symbol will never come into general use. Symbol is the manifestor of the thing signified, and if the thing signified has already existence, and if, by experience, we know that the symbol has expressed that thing many times, then we are sure that there is the real relation between them. Even if the things are not present, there will be thousands who will know them by their symbols. There must be a natural connection between the symbol and the thing signified; then, when that symbol is pronounced, it recalls the thing signified. The commentator says the manifesting word of God is *Om*. Why does he emphasize this? There are hundreds of words for God. One thought is connected with a thousand words; the idea, God, is connected with hundreds of words, and each one stands as a symbol for God. Very good. But there must be a generalisation among all these words, some substratum, some common ground of all these symbols, and that symbol which is the common symbol will be the best, and will really be the symbol of all. In making a sound we use the larynx, and the palate as a sounding board. Is there any material sound of which all other sounds must be manifestations, one which is the most natural sound? *Om* (*Aum*) is such a sound, the basis of all sounds. The first letter, A, is the root sound, the key, pronounced without touching any part of the tongue or palate; M represents the last sound in the series, being produced by the closed lips, and the U rolls from the very root to the end of the sounding board of the mouth. Thus, *Om* represents the whole phenomena of sound producing. As such, it must be the natural symbol, the matrix of all the various sounds. It denotes the whole range and possibility of all the words that can be made. Apart from these speculations we see that around this word *Om* are centred all the different religious ideas in India; all the various religious ideas of the *Vedas* have gathered themselves round this word *Om*. What has that to do with America and England, or any other country? Simply that the word has been retained at every stage of religious growth in India, and it has been manipulated to mean all the various ideas about God. Monists, Dualists, Mono-Dualists, Separatists, and even Atheists, took up this *Om*. *Om* has become the one symbol for the religious aspiration of the vast majority of human beings. Take, for instance, the English word God. It covers only a limited function, and, if you go beyond it, you have to add adjectives, to make it Personal, or Impersonal, or Absolute God. So with the words for God in every other language; their signification is very small. This word *Om*, however, has around it all the various significances. As such it should be accepted by everyone.

28. The repetition of this (Om) and meditating on its meaning (is the way).

Why should there be repetition? We have not forgotten that theory of *Samskâras*, that the sum-total of impressions lives in the mind. Impressions live in the mind, the sum-total of impressions, and they become more and more latent, but remain there, and as soon as they get the right stimulus they come out. Molecular vibration will never cease. When this universe is destroyed all the massive vibrations disappear, the sun, moon, stars, and earth, will melt down, but the vibrations must remain in the atoms. Each atom will perform the same function as the big worlds do. So the vibrations of this *Chitta* will subside, but will go on like molecular vibrations, and when they get the impulse will come out again. We can now understand what is meant by repetition. It is the greatest stimulus that can be given to the spiritual *Samskâras*. "One moment of company with the Holy makes a ship to cross this ocean of life." Such is the power of association. So this repetition of *Om*, and thinking of its meaning, is keeping good company in your own mind. Study, and then meditate and meditate, when you have studied. Thus light will come to you, the Self will become manifest.

But one must think of this *Om*, and of its meaning too. Avoid evil company, because the scars of old wounds are in you, and this evil company is just the heat that is necessary to call them out. In the same way we are told that good company will call out the good impressions that are in us, but which have become latent. There is nothing holier in this world than to keep good company, because the good impressions will have this same tendency to come to the surface.

29. From that is gained (the knowledge of) introspection, and the destruction of obstacles.

The first manifestation of this repetition and thinking of *Om* will be that the introspective power will be manifested more and more, and all the mental and physical obstacles will begin to vanish. What are the obstacles to the *Yogî?*

30. Disease, mental laziness, doubt, calmness, cessation, false perception, non-attaining concentration, and falling away from the state when obtained, are the obstructing distractions.

Disease. This body is the boat which will carry us to the other shore of the ocean of life. It must be taken care of. Unhealthy persons cannot be *Yogîs*. Mental laziness makes us lose all lively interest in the subject, without which there will neither be the will nor the energy to practise. Doubts will arise in the mind about the truth of the science, however strong one's intellectual conviction may be, until certain peculiar psychic experiences come, as hearing, or seeing, at a distance, etc. These glimpses strengthen the mind and make the student persevere. Falling away when attained. Some days or weeks when you are practising the mind will be calm and easily concentrated, and you will find yourself progressing fast. All of a sudden the progress will stop one day, and you will find yourself, as it were, stranded. Persevere. All progress proceeds by such rise and fall.

31. Grief, mental distress, tremor of the body, irregular breathing, accompany non-retention of concentration.

Concentration will bring perfect repose to mind and body every time it is practised. When the practice has been misdirected, or not enough controlled, these disturbances come. Repetition of *Om* and self-surrender to the Lord will strengthen the mind, and bring fresh energy. The nervous shakings will come to almost everyone. Do not mind them at all, but keep on practising. Practice will cure them, and make the seat firm.

32. To remedy this the practice of one subject (should be made).

Making the mind take the form of one object for some time will destroy these obstacles. This is general advice. In the following aphorisms it will be expanded and particularised. As one practice cannot suit everyone, various methods will be advanced, and everyone by actual experience will find out that which helps him most.

33. Friendship, mercy, gladness, indifference, being thought of in regard to subjects, happy, unhappy, good and evil respectively, pacify the Chitta.

We must have these four sorts of ideas. We must have friendship for all; we must be merciful towards those that are in misery; when people are happy we ought to be happy, and to the wicked we must be indifferent. So with all subjects that come before us. If the subject is a good one, we shall feel friendly towards it; if the subject of thought is one that is miserable we must be merciful towards the subject. If it is good we must be glad, if it is evil we must be indifferent. These attitudes of the mind towards the different subjects that come before it will make the mind peaceful. Most of our difficulties in our daily lives come from being unable to hold our minds in this way. For instance, if a man does evil to us, instantly we want to react evil, and every reaction of evil shows that we are not able to hold the *Chitta* down; it comes out in waves towards the object, and we lose our power. Every reaction in the form of hatred or evil is so much loss to the mind, and every evil thought or deed of hatred, or any thought of reaction, if it is controlled, will be laid in our favour. It is not that we lose by thus restraining ourselves; we are gaining infinitely more than we suspect. Each time we suppress hatred, or a feeling of anger, it is so much good energy stored up in our favour; that piece of energy will be converted into the higher powers.

34. By throwing out and restraining the Breath.

The word used is *Prâṇa*. *Prâṇa* is not exactly breath. It is the name for the energy that is in the universe. Whatever you see in the universe, whatever moves or works, or has life, is a manifestation of this

Prâṇa. The sum-total of the energy displayed in the universe is called *Prâṇa*. This *Prâṇa*, before a cycle begins, remains in an almost motionless state, and when the cycle begins this *Prâṇa* begins to manifest itself. It is this *Prâṇa* that is manifested as motion, as the nervous motion in human beings or animals, and the same *Prâṇa* is manifesting as thought, and so on. The whole universe is a combination of *Prâṇa* and *Âkâśa*; so is the human body. Out of *Âkâśa* you get the different materials that you feel, and see, and out of *Prâṇa* all the various forces. Now this throwing out and restraining the *Prâṇa* is what is called *Prâṇâyâma*. *Patanjali*, the father of the *Yoga* Philosophy, does not give very many particular directions about *Prâṇâyâma*, but later on other *Yogîs* found out various things about this *Prâṇâyâma*, and made of it a great science. With *Pantanjali* it is one of the many ways, but he does not lay much stress on it. He means that you simply throw the air out, and drawn it in, and hold it for some time, that is all, and by that, the mind will be come a little calmer. But, later on, you will find that out of this is evolved a particular science called *Prâṇâyâma*. We will hear a little of what these later *Yogîs* have to say. Some of this I have told you before, but a little repetition will serve to fix it in your minds. First, you must remember that this *Prâṇa* is not the breath. But that which causes the motion of the breath, that which is the vitality of the breath is the *Prâṇa*. Again, the word *Prâṇa* is used of all the senses; they are all called *Prâṇas*, the mind is called

Prâṇa; and so we see that *Prâṇa* is the name of a certain force. And yet we cannot call it force, because force is only the manifestation of it. It is that which manifests itself as force and everything else in the way of motion. The *Chitta*, the mind-stuff, is the engine which draws in the *Prâṇa* from the surroundings, and manufactures out of this *Prâṇa* these various vital forces. First of all the forces that keep the body in preservation, and lastly thought, will, and all other powers. By this process of breathing we can control all the various motions in the body, and the various nerve currents that are running through the body. First we begin to recognise them, and then we slowly get control over them. Now these later *Yogîs* consider that there are three main currents of this *Prâṇa* in the human body. One they call *Iḍâ*, another *Pingalâ*, and the third *Suṣumnâ*. *Pingalâ*, according to them, is on the right side of the spinal column, and the *Iḍâ* is on the left side, and in the middle of this spinal column is the *Suṣumnâ*, a vacant channel. *Iḍâ* and *Pingalâ*, according to them, are the currents working in every man, and through these currents, we are performing all the functions of life. *Suṣumnâ* is present in all, as a possibility; but it works only in the *Yogî*. You must remember that the *Yogî* changes his body; as you go on practising your body changes; it is not the same body that you had before the practice. That is very rational, and can be explained, because every new thought that we have must make, as it were, a new channel through the brain, and that explains the tremendous conservatism of human nature. Human nature likes to run through the ruts that are already there, because it is easy. If we think, just for example's sake, that the mind is like a needle, and the brain substance a soft lump before it, then each thought that we have makes a street, as it were, in the brain, and this street would close up, but that the grey matter comes and makes a lining to keep it separate. If there were no grey matter there would be no memory, because memory means going over these old streets, retracing a thought as it were. Now perhaps you have remarked that when I talk on subjects in which I take a few ideas that are familiar to everyone, and combine, and recombine them, it is easy to follow, because these channels are present in everyone's brain, and it is only necessary to recur to them. But whenever a new subject comes new channels have to be made, so it is not understood so readily. And that is why the brain (it is the brain, and not the people themselves) refuses unconsciously to be acted upon by new ideas. It resists. The *Prâṇa* is trying to make new channels, and the brain will not allow it. This is the secret of conservatism. The less channels there have been in the brain, and the less the needle of the *Prâṇa* has made these passages, the more conservative will be the brain, the more it will struggle against new thoughts. The more thoughtful the man, the more complicated will be the streets in his brain, and the more easily he will take to new ideas, and understand them. So with every fresh idea; we make a new impression in the brain, cut new channels through the brain-stuff, and that is why we find that in the practice of *Yoga* (it being an entirely new set of thoughts and motives) there is so much physical resistance at first. That is why we find that the part of religion which deals with the world side of nature can be so widely accepted, while the other part, the Philosophy, or the Psychology, which deals with the inner nature of man, is so frequently neglected. We must remember the definition of this world of ours; it is only the Infinite Existence projected into the plane of consciousness. A little of the Infinite is projected into consciousness, and that we call our world. So there is an Infinite beyond, and religion has to deal with both, with the little lump we call our world, and with the Infinite beyond. Any religion which deals alone with either one of these two will be defective. It must deal with both. That part of religion which deals with this part of the Infinite which has come into this plane of consciousness, got itself caught, as it were, in the plane of consciousness, in the cage of time, space, and causation, is quite familiar to us, because we are in that already, and ideas about this world have been with us almost from time immemorial. The part of religion which deals with the Infinite beyond comes entirely new to us, and getting ideas about it produces new channels in the brain, disturbing the whole system, and that is why you find in the practice of *Yoga* ordinary people are at first turned out of their grooves. In order to lessen these disturbances as much as possible all these methods are devised by *Patanjali*, that we may practise any one of them best suited to us.

35. Those forms of concentration that bring extraordinary sense perceptions cause perseverance of the mind.

This naturally comes with *Dhârâṇa*, concentration; the *Yogîs* say, if the mind becomes concentrated on the tip of the nose one begins to smell, after a few days, wonderful perfumes. If it becomes concentrated at the root of the tongue one begins to hear sounds; if on the tip of the tongue one begins to taste wonderful flavours; if on the middle of the tongue, one feels as if he were coming in contact with something. If one concentrates his mind on the palate he begins to see peculiar things. If a man whose mind is disturbed wants to take up some of these practices of *Yoga*, yet doubts the truth of them, he will have his doubts set at rest when, after a little practice, these things come to him, and he will persevere.

36. Or (by the meditation on) the Effulgent One which is beyond all sorrow.

This is another sort of concentration. Think of the lotus of the heart, with petals downwards, and running through it the *Suśumnâ*; take in the breath, and while throwing the breath out imagine that the lotus is turned with the petals upwards, and inside that lotus is an effulgent light. Meditate on that.

37. Or (by meditation on) the heart that has given up all attachment to sense objects.

Take some holy person, some great person whom you revere, some saint whom you know to be perfectly non-attached, and think of his heart. That heart has become non-attached, and meditate on that heart; it will calm the mind. If you cannot do that, there is the next way:

38. Or by meditating on the knowledge that comes in sleep.

Sometimes a man dreams that he has seen angels coming to him and talking to him, that he is in an ecstatic condition, that he has heard music floating through the air. He is in a blissful condition in that dream, and when he awakes it makes a deep impression on him. Think of that dream as real, and meditate upon it. If you cannot do that, meditate on any holy thing that pleases you.

39. Or by the meditation on anything that appeals to one as good.

This does not mean any wicked subject, but anything good that you like, any place that you like best, any scenery that you like best, any idea that you like best, anything that will concentrate the mind.

40. The Yogi's mind thus meditating, becomes unobstructed from the atomic to the Infinite.

The mind, by this practice, easily contemplates the most minute thing, as well as the biggest thing. Thus the mind waves become fainter.

41. The Yogi whose Vṛittis have thus become powerless (controlled) obtains in the receiver, receiving, and received (the self, the mind and external objects), concentratedness and sameness, like the crystal (before different coloured objects.)

What results from this constant meditation? We must remember how in a previous aphorism *Patanjali* went into the various states of meditation, and how the first will be the gross, and the second the fine objects, and from them the advance is to still finer objects of meditation, and how, in all these meditations, which are only of the first degree, not very high ones, we get as a result that we can meditate as easily on the fine as on the grosser objects. Here the *Yogí* sees the three things, the receiver, the received, and the receiving, corresponding to the Soul, the object, and the mind. There are three objects of meditation given us. First the gross things, as bodies, or material objects, second fine things, as the mind, the *Chitta*, and third the *Puruṡa* qualified, not the *Puruṣa* itself, but the egosim. By practice, the *Yogí* gets established in all these meditations. Whenever he meditates he can keep out all other thought; he becomes identified with that on which he meditates; when he meditates he is like a piece of crystal; before flowers the crystal becomes almost identified with the flowers. If the flower is red, the crystal looks red, or if the flower is blue, the crystal looks blue.

42. Sound, meaning, and resulting knowledge, being mixed up, is (called Samâdhi) with reasoning.

Sound here means vibration; meaning, the nerve currents which conduct it; and knowledge, reaction. All the various meditations we have had so far, *Patanjali* calls *Savitarka* (meditations with reasoning). Later on he will give us higher and higher *Dhyânas*. In these that are called "with reasoning," we keep the dualty of subject and object, which results from the mixture of word, meaning, and knowledge. There is first the external vibration, the word; this, carried inward by the sense currents, is the meaning. After that there comes a reactionary wave in the *Chitta*, which is knowledge, but the mixture of these three make up what we call knowledge. In all the meditations up to this we get this mixture as object of meditation. The next *Samâdhi* is higher.

43. The Samâdhi called without reasoning (comes) when the memory is purified, or devoid of qualities, expressing only the meaning (of the meditated object).

It is by practice of meditation of these three that we come to the state where these three do not mix. We can get rid of them. We will first try to understand what these three are. Here is the *Chitta;* you will always remember the simile of the lake, the mind-stuff, and the vibration, the word, the sound, like a pulsation coming over it. You have that calm lake in you, and I pronounce a word, "cow." As soon as it enters through your ears there is a wave produced in your *Chitta* along with it. So that wave represents the idea of the cow, the form or the meaning as we call it. That apparent cow that you know is really that wave in the mind-stuff, and that comes as a reaction to the internal and external sound vibrations, and with the sound, the wave dies away; that wave can never exist without a word. You may ask how it is when we only think of the cow, and do not hear a sound. You make that sound yourself. You are saying "cow" faintly in your mind, and with that comes a wave. There cannot be any wave without this impulse of sound, and when it is not from outside it is from inside, and when the sound dies, the wave dies. What remains? The result of the reaction, and that is knowledge. These three are so closely combined in our mind that we cannot separate them. When the sound comes, the senses vibrate, and the wave rises in reaction; they follow so closely upon one another that there is no discerning one from the other; when this meditation has been practised for a long time, memory, the receptacle of all impressions, becomes purified, and we are able clearly to distinguish them from one another. This is called "*Nirvitarka,*" concentration without reasoning.

44. By this process (the concentrations) with discrimination and without discrimination, whose objects are finer, are (also) explained.

A process similar to the preceding is applied again, only, the objects to be taken up in the former meditations are gross; in this they are fine.

45. The finer objects end with the Pradhâna.

The gross objects are only the elements, and everything manufactured out of them. The fine objects begin with the *Tanmatras* or fine particles. The organs, the mind,* egoism, the mind-stuff (the cause of all manifestation) the equilibrium state of *Sattva*, *Rajas* and *Tamas* materials — called *Pradhâna* (chief), *Prakriti* (nature), or *Avyakta* (unmanifest), are all included within the category of fine objects. The *Puruṣa* (the Soul) alone is excepted from this definition.

46. These concentrations are with seed.

These do not destroy the seeds of past actions, thus cannot give liberation, but what they bring to the *Yogî* is stated in the following aphorisms.

47. The concentration "without reasoning" being purified, the Chitta becomes firmly fixed.

48. The knowledge in that is called "filled with Truth."

The next aphorism will explain this.

* The mind or common sensory, the aggregate of all senses.

49. The knowledge that is gained from testimony and inference is about common objects. That from the Samâdhi just mentioned is of a much higher order, being able to penetrate where inference and testimony cannot go.

The idea is that we have to get our knowledge of ordinary objects by direct perception, and by inference therefrom, and from testimony of people who are competent. By "people who are competent," the *Yogîs* always mean the *Rishîs*, or the Seers of the thoughts recorded in the Scriptures — the *Vedas*. According to them, the only proof of the Scriptures is that they were the testimony of competent persons, yet they say the Scriptures cannot take us to realisation. We can read all the *Vedas*, and yet will not realise anything, but when we practise their teachings, then we attain to that state which realises what the Scriptures say, which penetrates where reason cannot go, and where neither perception nor inference can go, and where the testimony of others cannot avail. This is what is meant by this aphorism, that realisation is real religion, and all the rest is only preparation — hearing lectures, or reading books, or reasoning, is merely preparing the ground; it is not religion. Intellectual assent, and intellectual dissent are not religion. The central idea of the *Yogîs* is that just as we come in direct contact with objects of the senses, so religion even can be directly perceived in a far more intense sense. The truths of religion, as God and Soul, cannot be perceived by the external senses. I cannot see God with my eyes, nor can I touch Him with my hands, and we also know that neither can we reason beyond the senses. Reason leaves us at a point quite indecisive; we may reason all our lives, as the world has been doing for thousands of years, and the result is that we find we are incompetent to prove or disprove the facts of religion. What we perceive directly we take as the basis, and upon that basis we reason. So it is obvious that reasoning has to run within these bounds of perception. It can never go beyond; the whole scope of realisation, therefore, is beyond sense perception. The *Yogîs* say that man can go beyond his direct sense perception, and beyond his reason also. Man has in him the faculty, the power, of transcending his intellect even, and that power is in every being, every creature. By the practice of *Yoga* that power is aroused, and then man transcends the ordinary limits of reason, and directly perceives things which are beyond all reason.

50. The resulting impression from this Samâdhi obstructs all other impressions.

We have seen in the foregoing aphorism that the only way of attaining to that super-consciousness is by concentration, and we have also seen that what hinder the mind from concentration are the past *Samskâras*, impressions. All of you have observed that when you are trying to concentrate your mind, your thoughts wander. When you are trying to think of God, that is the very time which all these *Samskâras* take to appear.

At other times they are not so active, but when you want them not to be they are sure to be there, trying their best to crowd inside your mind. Why should that be so? Why should they be much more potent at the time of concentration? It is because you are repressing them and they react with all their force. At other times they do not react. How countless these old past impressions must be, all lodged somewhere in the *Chitta*, ready, waiting like tigers to jump up. These have to be suppressed that the one idea which we like may arise, to the exclusion of the others. Instead, they are all struggling to come up at the same time. These are the various powers of the *Samskâras* in hindering concentration of the mind, so this *Samâdhi* which has just been given is the best to be practised, on account of its power of suppressing the *Samskâras*. The *Samskâra* which will be raised by this sort of concentration will be so powerful that it will hinder the action of the others, and hold them in check.

51 By the restraint of even this (impression, which obstructs all other impressions), all being restrained, comes the "seedless" Samâdhi.

You remember that our goal is to perceive the Soul itself. We cannot perceive the Soul because it has got mingled up with nature, with the mind, with the body. The most ignorant man thinks his body is the Soul. The more learned man thinks his mind is the Soul, but both of these are mistaken. What makes the Soul get mingled up with all this, these different waves

10

in the *Chitta* rise and cover the Soul, and we only see a little reflection of the Soul through these waves, so, if the wave is one of anger, we see the Soul as angry; "I am angry," we say. If the wave is a wave of love we see ourselves reflected in that wave, and say we are loving. If that wave is one of weakness, and the Soul is reflected in it, we think we are weak. These various ideas come from these impressions, these *Samskâras* covering the Soul. The real nature of the Soul is not perceived as long as there is one single wave in the lake of the *Chitta*, this real nature will never be perceived until all the waves have subsided; so, first, *Patanjali* teaches us the meaning of these waves; secondly, the best way to repress them; and thirdly, how to make one wave so strong as to suppress all other waves, fire eating fire as it were. When only one remains it will be easy to suppress that also, and when that is gone, this *Samâdhi* of concentration is called seedless; it leaves nothing, and the Soul is manifested just as It is, in Its own glory. Then alone we know that the Soul is not a compound, It is the only eternal simple in the universe, and, as such, It cannot be born, It cannot die, It is immortal, indestructible, the Ever living Essence of intelligence.

CHAPTER II.

CONCENTRATION — ITS PRACTICE.

1. Mortification, study, and surrendering fruits of work to God are called Kriya Yoga.

Those *Samâdhis* with which we ended our last chapter are very difficult to attain; so we must take them up slowly. The first step, the preliminary step, is called *Kriya Yoga*. Literally this means work, working towards *Yoga*. The organs are the horses, the mind is the reins, the intellect is the charioteer, the soul is the rider, and this body is the chariot. The master of the household, the King, the Self of man, is sitting in this chariot. If the horses are very strong, and do not obey the reins, if the charioteer, the intellect, does not know how to control the horses, then this chariot will come to grief. But if the organs, the horses, are well controlled, and if the reins, the mind, are well held in the hands of the charioteer, the intellect, the chariot reaches the goal. What is meant, therefore, by this mortification? Holding the reins firmly while guiding this body and mind; not letting the body do anything it likes, but keeping them both in proper control. Study. What is meant by study in this case? Not study of novels, or fiction, or story books, but study of those books which teach the liberation of the soul.

Then again this study does not mean controversial studies at all. The *Yogî* is supposed to have finished his period of controversy. He has had enough of that, and has become satisfied. He only studies to intensify his convictions. *Vâda* and *Siddhânta.* These are the two sorts of Scriptural knowledge, *Vâda* (the argumentative) and *Siddhânta* (the decisive). When a man is entirely ignorant he takes up the first part of this, the argumentative fighting, and reasoning, *pro* and *con.*; and when he has finished that he takes up the *Siddhânta*, the decisive, arriving at a conclusion. Simply arriving at this conclusion will not do. It must be intensified. Books are infinite in number, and time is short; therefore this is the secret of knowledge, to take that which is essential. Take that out, and then try to live up to it. There is an old simile in India that if you place a cup of milk before a *Râja Hamsa* (swan) with plenty of water in it, he will take all the milk and leave the water. In that way we should take what is of value in knowledge, and leave the dross. All these intellectual gymnastics are necessary at first. We must not go blindly into anything. The *Yogî* has passed the argumentative stage, and has come to a conclusion, which is like the rocks, immovable. The only thing he now seeks to do is to intensify that conclusion. Do not argue, he says; if one forces arguments upon you, be silent. Do not answer any argument, but go away free, because arguments only disturb the mind. The only thing is to train the intellect, so what is the use of disturbing it any more. The intellect is but a weak instrumens and can give us only knowledge limited by the senses; the *Yogî* wants to go beyond the senses; therefore intellect is of no use to him. He is certain of this, and therefore is silent, and does not argue. Every argument throws his mind out of balance, creates a disturbance in the *Chitta*, and this disturbance is a drawback. These argumentations and searchings of the reason are only on the way. There are much higher things behind them. The whole of life is not for schoolboy fights and debating societies. "By surrendering the fruits of work to God" is to take to ourselves neither credit not blame, but to give both up to the Lord, and be at peace.

2. (They are for) the practice of Samâdhi and minimizing the pain-bearing obstructions.

Most of us make our minds like spoiled children, allowing them to do whatever they want. Therefore it is necessary that there should be constant practice of the previous mortifications, in order to gain control of the mind, and bring it into subjection. The obstructions to *Yoga* arise from lack of this control, and cause us pain. They can only be removed by denying the mind, and holding it in check, through these various means.

3. The pain-bearing obstructions are — ignorance, egoism, attachment, aversion, and clinging to life.

These are the five pains, the fivefold tie that binds us down. Of course ignorance is the mother of all the rest. She is the only cause of all our misery. What else can make us miserable? The nature of the Soul is eternal bliss. What can make it sorrowful except ignorance, hallucination, delusion; all this pain of the soul is simply delusion.

4. Ignorance is the productive field of all these that follow, whether they are dormant, attenuated, overpowered, or expanded.

Impressions are the cause of these, and these impressions exist in different degrees. There are the dormant. You often hear the expression "innocent as a baby," yet in the baby may be the state of a demon or of a god, which will come out by and by. In the *Yogî*, these impressions, the *Samskâras* left by past actions, are attenuated; that is, in a very fine state, and he can control them, and not allow them to become manifest. Overpowered means that sometimes one set of impressions is held down for awhile by those that are stronger, but they will come out when that repressing cause is removed. The last state is the expanded, when the *Samskâras*, having helpful surroundings, have attained to great activity, either as good or evil.

5. Ignorance is taking that which is non-eternal, impure, painful, and non-Self, for the eternal, pure, happy, Âtman (Self).

All these various sorts of impressions have one source, ignorance. We have first to learn what ignorance is.

All of us think that "I am the body," and not the Self, the pure, the effulgent, the ever blissful, and that is ignorance. We think of man, and see man as body. This is the great delusion.

6. Egoism is the identification of the seer with the instrument of seeing.

The seer is really the Self, the pure one, the ever holy, the infinite, the immortal. That is the Self of man. And what are the instruments? The *Chitta*, or mind-stuff, the *Buddhi*, determinative faculty, the *Manas*, or mind, and the *Indriyâṇi*, or sense organs. These are the instruments for him to see the external world, and the identification of the Self with the instruments is what is called the ignorance of egoism. We say "I am the mind, I am thought; I am angry, or I am happy." How can we be angry, and how can we hate? We should identify ourselves with the Self; that cannot change. If it is unchangeable, how can it be one moment happy, and one moment unhappy? It is formless, infinite, omnipresent. What can change it? Beyond all law. What can affect it? Nothing in the universe can produce an effect on it, yet, through ignorance, we identify ourselves with the mind-stuff, and think we feel pleasure or pain.

7. Attachment is that which dwells on pleasure.

We find pleasure in certain things, and the mind, like a current, flows towards them, and that, following the pleasure centre, as it were, is attachment. We are never attached to anyone in whom we do not find pleasure. We find pleasure in very queer things sometimes, but the definition is just the same; wherever we find pleasure, there we are attached.

8. Aversion is that which dwells on pain.

That which gives us pain we immediately seek to get away from.

9. Flowing through its own nature, and established even in the learned, is the clinging to life.

This clinging to life you see manifested in every animal, and upon it many attempts have been made to build the theory of a future life, because men like their lives so much that they desire a future life also. Of course it goes without saying that this argument is without much value, but the most curious part of it is that, in Western Countries, the idea that this clinging to life indicates a possibility of a future life applies only to men, but does not include animals. In India this clinging to life has been one of the arguments to prove past experience and existence. For instance, if it be true that all our knowledge has come from experience, then it is sure that that which we never experienced we cannot imagine, or understand. As soon as chickens are hatched they begin to pick up food. Many times it has been seen where ducks have been hatched by hens, that, as soon as they come out of the eggs, they flew to water, and the mother thought they would be drowned. If experience be the only source of knowledge, where did these chickens learn to pick up food, or the ducklings that the water was their natural element? If you say it is instinct, it means nothing — it is simply giving a word, but is no explanation. What is this instinct? We have many instincts in ourselves. For instance, most of you ladies play the piano, and remember, when you first learned, how carefully you had to put your fingers on the black and the white keys, one after the other, but now, after long years of practice, you can talk with your friends, and your hand goes on just the same. It has become instinct. So with every work we do; by practice it becomes instinct, it becomes automatic, but so far as we know, all the cases which we now regard as automatic, are degenerated reason. In the language of the *Yogî*, instinct is involved reason. Discrimination becomes involved, and gets to be automatic *Samskâras*. Therefore it is perfectly logical to think that all we call instinct in this world is simply involved reason. As reason cannot come without experience, all instinct is, therefore, the result of past experience. Chickens fear the hawk, and ducklings love the water, and these are both the result of past experience. Then the question is whether that experience belongs to a particular soul, or to the body simply, whether this experience which comes to the duck is the duck's forefather's experience, or the duck's own experience. Modern scientific men hold that it belongs to the body, but the *Yogîs* hold that it is the experience of the mind, transmitted through the body. This is called the theory of reincarnation. We have seen that all our knowledge, whether we call it perception or reason, or instinct, must come through that one channel called experience, and all that we now call instinct is the result of past experience, degenerated into instinct, and that instinct regenerates into reason again. So on throughout the universe, and upon this has been built one of the chief arguments for reincarnation, in India. The recurring experiences of various fears, in course of time, produce this clinging to life. That is why the child is instinctively afraid, because the past experience of pain is there. Even in the most learned men, who know that this body will go, and who say "never mind; we have hundreds of bodies; the soul cannot die"—even in them, with all their intellectual convictions, we still find this clinging on to life. What is this clinging to life? We have seen that it has become instinctive. In the psychological language of the *Yogîs* it has become *Samskâras*. The *Samskâras*, fine and hidden, are sleeping in the *Chitta*. All these past experiences of death, all that which we call instinct, is experience become sub-conscious. It lives in the *Chitta*, and is not inactive, but is working underneath. These *Chitta Vṛittis*, these mind-waves, which are gross, we can appreciate and feel; they can be more easily controlled, but what about these finer instincts? How can they be controlled? When I am angry my whole mind has become a huge wave of anger. I feel it, see it, handle it, can easily manipulate it, can fight with it, but I shall not succeed perfectly in the fight until I can get down below. A man says something very harsh to me, and I begin to feel that I am getting heated, and he goes on till I am perfectly angry, and forget myself, identify myself with anger. When he first began to abuse me I still thought "I am going to be angry." Anger was one thing and I was another, but when I became angry, I was anger. These feelings have to be controlled in the germ, the root, in their fine forms, before even we have become conscious that they are acting on us. With the vast majority of mankind the fine states of these passions are not even known, the state when they are slowly coming from beneath consciousness. When a bubble is rising from the bottom of the lake we do not see it, or even when it is nearly come to the surface; it is only when it bursts and makes a ripple that we know it is there. We shall only be successful in grappling with the waves when we can get hold of them in their fine causes, and until you can get hold of them, and subdue them before they become gross, there is no hope of conquering any passion perfectly. To control our passions we have to control them at their very roots; then alone shall we be able to burn out their very seeds. As fried seeds thrown into the ground will never come up, so these passions will never arise.

10. They, to-be-rejected-by-opposite-modifications, are fine.

How are these fine *Samskâras* to be controlled? We have to begin with the big waves, and come down and down. For instance, when a big wave of anger has come into the mind, how are we to control that? Just by raising a big opposing wave. Think of love. Sometimes a mother is very angry with her husband, and while in that state the baby comes in, and she kisses the baby; the old wave dies out, and a new wave arises, love for the child. That suppresses the other one. Love is opposite to anger. So we find that by raising the opposite waves we can conquer those which we want to reject. Then, if we can raise in our fine nature these fine opposing waves, they will check the fine workings of anger beneath the conscious surface. We have seen now that all these instinctive actions first began as conscious actions, and became finer and finer. So, if good waves in the conscious *Chitta* be constantly raised, they will go down, become subtle, and oppose the *Samskâra* forms of evil thoughts.

11. By meditation, their modifications are to be rejected.

Meditation is one of the great means of controlling the rising of these big waves. By meditation you can make the mind subdue these waves, and, if you go on practising meditation for days, and months, and years, until it has become a habit, until it will come in spite of yourself, anger and hatred will be controlled and checked.

12. The receptacle of works has its root in these pain-bearing obstructions, and their experience in this visible life, or in the unseen life.

By the receptacle of works is meant the sum-total of these *Samskâras*. Whatever work we do, the mind is thrown into a wave, and, after the work is finished, we think the wave is gone. No. It has only become fine, but it is still there. When we try to remember the thing, it comes up again and becomes a wave. So it was there; if it had not been there, there would not have been memory. So, every action, every thought, good or bad, just goes down and becomes fine, and is there stored up. They are called pain-bearing obstructions, both happy and unhappy thoughts, because according to the *Yogís*, both, in the long run, bring pain. All happiness which comes from the senses will, eventually, bring pain. All enjoyment will make us thirst for more, and that brings pain as its result. There is no limit to man's desires; he goes on desiring, and when he comes to a point where desire cannot be fulfilled, the result is pain. Therefore the *Yogís* regard the sum-total of the impressions, good or evil, as pain-bearing obstructions; they obstruct the way to freedom of the Soul. It is the same with the *Samskâras*, the fine roots of all our works; they are the causes which will again bring effects, either in this life, or in the lives to come. In exceptional cases, when these *Samskâras* are very strong, they bear fruit quickly; exceptional acts of wickedness, or of goodness, bring their fruits in this life. The *Yogîs* even hold that men who are able to acquire a tremendous power of good *Samskâras* do not have to die, but, even in this life, can change their bodies into god-bodies. There are several cases mentioned by the *Yogîs* in their books. These men change the very material of their bodies; they re-arrange the molecules in such fashion that they have no more sickness, and what we call death does not come to them. Why should not this be? The physiological meaning of food is assimilation of energy from the sun. This energy has reached the plant, the plant is eaten by an animal, and the animal by us. The science of it is that we take so much energy from the sun, and make it part of ourselves. That being the case, why should there be only one way of assimilating energy? The plant's way is not the same as ours; the earth's process of assimilating energy differs from our own. But all assimilate energy in some form or other. The *Yogîs* say that they are able to assimilate energy by the power of the mind alone, that they can draw in as much as they desire without recourse to the ordinary methods. As a spider makes his net out of his own substance, and becomes bound in his net, and cannot go anywhere except along the lines of that net, so we have projected out of our own substance this net-work called the nerves, and we cannot work except through the channels of those nerves. The *Yogî* says we need not be bound by that.

Similarly, we can send electricity to any part of the world, but we have to send it by means of wires. Nature can send a vast mass of electricity without any wires at all. Why cannot we do the same? We can send mental electricity. What we call mind is very much the same as electricity. It is clear that this nerve fluid has some amount of electricity, because it is polarised, and it answers all electrical directions. We can only send our electricity through these nerve channels. Why not send the mental electricity without this aid? The *Yogî* says it is perfectly possible and practicable, and that when you can do that you will work all over the universe. You will be able to work with any body anywhere, without the help of any nervous system. When the soul is acting through these channels we say a man is living and when those channels die the man is said to be dead. But when a man is able to act either with or without these channels, birth and death will have no meaning for him. All the bodies in the universe are made up of *Tanmâtras*, and it is only in the arrangement of them that there comes a difference. If you are the arranger you can arrange that body in one way or another. Who makes up this body but you? Who eats the food? If another ate the food for you you would not live long. Who makes the blood out of it? You, certainly. Who assimilates the blood, and sends it through the veins? You. Who creates the nerves, and makes all the muscles? You are the manufacturer, out of your own substance. You are the manufacturer of the body, and you live in it. Only we have lost the knowledge of how to make it. We have become automatic, degenerate. We have forgotten the process of manufacture. So, what we do automatically has again to be regulated. We are the creators and we have to regulate that creation, and as soon as we can do that we shall be able to manufacture just as we like, and then we shall have neither birth nor death, disease, or anything.

13. The root being there, the fruition comes (in the form of) species, life, and experience of pleasure and pain.

The roots, the causes, the *Samskâras* being there, they again manifest, and form the effects. The cause dying down becomes the effect, and the effect becomes more subtle, and becomes the cause of the next effect. The tree bears a seed, and becomes the cause of the next tree, and so on. All our works now, are the effects of past *Samskâras*. Again, these *Samskâras* become the cause of future actions, and thus we go on. So this aphorism says that the cause being there, the fruit must come, in the form of species; one will be a man, another an angel, another an animal, another a demon. Then there are different effects in life; one man lives fifty years, another a hundred, and another dies in two years, and never attains maturity; all these differences in life are regulated by these past actions. One man is born, as it were, for pleasure; if he buries himself in a forest pleasure will follow him there.

Another man, wherever he goes, pain follows him; everything becomes painful. It is all the result of their own past. According to the philosophy of the *Yogîs* all virtuous actions bring pleasure, and all vicious actions bring pain. Any man who does wicked deeds is sure to reap the fruit of them in the form of pain.

14. They bear fruit as pleasure or pain, caused by virtue or vice.

15. To the discriminating, all is, as it were, painful on account of everything bringing pain, either in the consequence, or in apprehension, or in attitude caused by impressions, also on account of the counter action of qualities.

The *Yogîs* say that the man who has discriminating powers, the man of good sense, sees through all these various things, which are called pleasure and pain, and knows that they are always equally distributed, and that one follows the other, and melts into the other; he sees that men are following an *ignis fatuus* all their lives, and never succeed in fulfilling their desires. There was never a love in this world which did not know decay. The great king *Yudiṣṭhira* once said that the most wonderful thing in life is that every moment we see people dying around us, and yet we think we shall never die. Surrounded by fools on every side, we think we are the only exceptions, the only learned men. Surrounded by all sorts of experiences of fickleness, we think our love is the only lasting love. How can that be? Even love is selfish, and the *Yogî* says that, in the end, we shall find that even the love of husbands and wives, and children and friends, slowly decays. Decadence seizes everything in this life. It is only when everything, even love, fails, that, with a flash, man finds out how vain, how dream-like is this world. Then he catches a glimpse of *Vairâgyam* (renunciation), catches a glimpse of the beyond. It is only by giving up this world that the other comes; never through holding on to this one. Never yet was there a great soul who had not to reject sense pleasures and enjoyments to become such. The cause of misery is the clash between the different forces of nature, one dragging one way, and another dragging another, rendering permanent happiness impossible.

16. The misery which is not yet come is to be avoided.

Some *Karma* we have worked out already, some we are working out now in the present, and some is waiting to bear fruit in the future. That which we have worked out already is past and gone.

That which we are experiencing now we will have to work out, and it is only that which is waiting to bear fruit in the future that we can conquer and control, so all our forces should be directed towards the control of that *Karma* which has not yet borne fruit. That is meant in the previous aphorism, when *Patanjali* says that these various *Samskâras* are to be controlled by counteracting waves.

17. The cause of that which is to be avoided is the junction of the seer and the seen.

Who is the seer? The Self of Man, the *Puruṣa.* What is the seen? The whole of nature, beginning with the mind, down to gross matter. All this pleasure and pain arises from the junction between this *Puruṣa* and the mind. The *Puruṣa*, you must remember, according to this philosophy, is pure; it is when it is joined to nature, and by reflection, that it appears to feel either pleasure or pain.

18. The experienced is composed of elements and organs, is of the nature of illumination, action and inertia, and is for the purpose of experience and release (of the experiencer).

The experienced, that is nature, is composed of elements and organs — the elements gross and fine which compose the whole of nature, and the organs of the senses, mind, etc., and is of the nature of illumination, action, and inertia. These are what in Sanskrit are called *Sattva* (illumination), *Rajas* (action), and *Tamas* (inertia); each is for the purpose of experience and release. What is the purpose of the whole of nature? That the *Puruṣa* may gain experience. The *Puruṣa* has, as it were, forgotten its mighty, godly nature. There is a story that the king of the gods, *Indra*, once became a pig, wallowing in mire; he had a she pig, and a lot of baby pigs, and was very happy. Then some other angels saw his plight, and came to him, and told him, "You are the king of the gods, you have all the gods command. Why are you here?" But *Indra* said, "Let me be; I am all right here; I do not care for the heavens, while I have this sow and these little pigs." The poor gods were at their wits' end what to do. After a time they decided to slowly come and slay one of the little pigs, and then another, until they had slain all the pigs, and the sow too. When all were dead *Indra* began to weep and mourn. Then the gods ripped his pig body open and he came out of it, and began to laugh when he realised what a hideous dream he had had; he, the king of the gods, to have become a pig, and to think that that pig-life was the only life! Not only so, but to have wanted the whole universe to come into the pig life! The *Puruśa*, when it identifies itself with nature, forgets that it is pure and infinite. The *Puruṣa* does not live; it is life itself. It does not exist; it is existence itself. The Soul does not know; it is knowledge itself. It is an entire mistake to say the Soul lives, or knows, or loves. Love and existence are not the qualities of the *Puruṣa*, but its essence. When they get reflected upon something you may call them the qualities of that something. But they are not the qualities of the *Puruṣa*, but the essence of this great *Âtman*, this Infinite Being, without birth or death, Who is established in His own glory, but appears as if become degenerate until if you approach to tell Him, "You are not a pig," he begins to squeal and bite. Thus with us all in this *Mâyâ*, this dream world, where it is all misery, weeping, and crying, where a few golden balls are rolled, and the world scrambles after them. You were never bound by laws, Nature never had a bond for you. That is what the *Yogî* tells you; have patience to learn it. And the *Yogî* shows how, by junction with this nature, and identifying itself with the mind and the world, the *Puruṣa* thinks itself miserable. Then the *Yogî* goes on to show you that the way out is through experience. You have to get all this experience, but finish it quickly. We have placed ourselves in this net, and will have to get out. We have got ourselves caught in the trap, and we will have to work out our freedom. So get this experience of husbands and wives, and friends, and little loves, and you will get through them safely if you never forget what you really are. Never forget this is only a momentary state, and that we have to pass through it. Experience is the one great teacher — experiences of pleasure and pain — but know they are only experiences, and will all lead, step by step, to that state when all these things will become small, and the *Puruṣa* will be so great that this whole universe will be as a drop in the ocean, and will fall off by its own nothingness. We have to go through these experiences, but let us never forget the ideal.

19. The states of the qualities are the defined, the undefined, the indicated only, and the signless.

The system of *Yoga* is built entirely on the philosophy of the *Sânkhyas*, as I told you in some of the previous lectures, and here again I will remind you of the cosmology of the *Sânkhya* philosophy. According to the *Sânkhyas*, nature is both the material and the efficient cause of this universe. In this nature there are three sorts of materials, the *Sattva*, the *Rajas*, and the *Tamas*. The *Tamas* material is all that is dark, all that is ignorant and heavy; and the *Rajas* is activity. The *Sattva* is calmness, light. When nature is in the state before creation, it is called by them *Avyaktam*, undefined, or indiscrete; that is, in which there is no distinction of form or name, a state in which these three materials are held in perfect balance. Then the balance is disturbed, these different materials begin to mingle in various fashions, and the result is this universe. In every man, also, these three materials exist. When the *Sattva* material prevails knowledge comes. When the *Rajas* material prevails activity comes, and when the *Tamas* material prevails darkness comes, and lassitude, idleness, ignorance. According to the *Sânkhya* theory, the highest manifestation of this nature, consisting of these three materials, is what they call *Mahat*, or intelligence, universal intelligence, and each human mind is a part of that cosmic intelligence. Then out of *Mahat* comes the mind. In the *Sânkhya* Psychology there is a sharp distinction between *Manas*, the mind function, and the function of the *Buddhi* intellect. The mind function is simply to collect and carry impressions and present them to the *Buddhi*, the individual *Mahat*, and the *Buddhi* determines upon it. So, out of *Mahat* comes mind, and out of mind comes fine material, and this fine material combines and becomes the gross material outside — the external universe. The claim of the *Sânkhya* philosophy is that beginning with the intellect, and coming down to a block of stone, all has come out of the same thing, only as finer or grosser states of existence. The *Buddhi* is the finest state of existence of the materials, and then comes *Ahamkâra*, egoism, and next to the mind comes fine material, which they call *Tanmâtras*, which cannot be seen, but which are inferred. These *Tanmâtras* combine and become grosser, and finally produce this universe. The finer is the cause, and the grosser is the effect. It begins with the *Buddhi*, which is the finest material, and goes on becoming grosser and grosser, until it becomes this universe. According to the *Sânkhya* philosophy, beyond the whole of nature is the *Puruṣa*, which is not material at all. *Puruṣa* is not at all similar to anything else, either *Buddhi*, or mind, or the *Tanmâtras*, or the gross material; it is not akin to any one of these, it is entirely separate, entirely different in its nature, and from this they argue that the *Puruṣa* must be immortal, because it is not the result of combination. That which is not the result of combination cannot die, these *Puruṣas* or Souls are infinite in number. Now we shall understand the Aphorism, that the states of the qualities are defined, undefined, and signless. By the defined is meant the gross elements, which we can sense. By the undefined is meant the very fine materials, the *Tanmâtras*, which cannot be sensed by ordinary men. If you practice *Yoga*, however, says *Patanjali*, after a while your perceptions will become so fine that you will actually see the *Tanmâtras*. For instance, you have heard how every man has a certain light about him; every living being is emanating a certain light, and this, he says, can be seen by the *Yogî*. We do not all see it, but we are all throwing out these *Tanmâtras*, just as a flower is continuously emanating these *Tanmâtras*, which enable us to smell it. Every day of our lives we are throwing out a mass of good or evil, and everywhere we go the atmosphere is full of these materials, and that is how there came to the human mind, even unconsciously, the idea of building temples and churches. Why should man build churches in which to worship God? Why not worship Him anywhere? Even if he did not know the reason, man found that that place where people worshipped God became full of good *Tanmâtras*. Every day people go there, and the more they go the holier they get, and the holier that place becomes. If any man who has not much *Sattva* in him goes there the place will influence him, and arouse his *Sattva* quality. Here, therefore, is the significance of all temples and holy places, but you must remember that their holiness depends on holy people congregating there. The difficulty with mankind is that they forget the original meaning, and put the cart before the horse. It was men who made these places holy, and then the effect became the cause and made men holy. If the wicked only were to go there it would become as bad as any other place. It is not the building, but the people, that make a church, and that is what we always forget. That is why sages and holy persons, who have so much of this *Sattva* quality, are emanating so much of it around them, and exerting a tremendous influence day and night on their surroundings. A man may become so pure that his purity will become tangible, as it were. The body has become pure, and in an intensely physical sense, no figurative idea, no poetical language, it emanates that purity wherever it goes. Whosoever comes in contact with that man becomes pure. Next "the indicated only" means the *Buddhi*, the intellect. "The indicated only" is the first manifestation of nature; from it all other manifestations proceed. The last is "the signless." Here there seems to be a great fight between modern science and all religions. Every religion has this idea that this universe comes out of intelligence. Only some religions were more philosophical, and used scientific language. The very theory of God, taking it in its psychological significance, and apart from all ideas of personal God, is that intelligence is first in the order of creation, and that out of intelligence comes what we call gross matter. Modern philosophers say that intelligence is the last to come. They say that unintelligent things slowly evolve into animals, and from animals slowly evolve into men. They claim that instead of everything coming out of intelligence, intelligence is itself the last to come. Both the religious and the scientific statement, though seeming directly opposed to each other, are true. Take an infinite series, A—B—A—B—A—B, etc. The question is which is first, A or B. If you take the series as A—B, you will say that A is first, but if you take it as B—A you will say that B is first. It depends upon the way we are looking at it. Intelligence evolves, and becomes the gross matter, and this again involves as intelligence, and again evolves as matter once more. The *Sânkhyas*, and all religionists, put intelligence first, and the series becomes intelligence then matter, intelligence then matter. The scientific man puts his finger on matter, and says matter then intelligence, matter then intelligence. But they are both indicating the same chain. Indian philosophy, however, goes beyond both intelligence and matter, and finds a *Puruṣa*, or Self, which is beyond all intelligence, and of which intelligence is but the borrowed light.

20. The seer is intelligence only, and though pure, sees through the colouring of the intellect.

This is again *Sânkhya* philosophy. We have seen from this philosophy that from the lowest form up to intelligence all is nature, but beyond nature are *Puruṣas* (souls), and these have no qualities. Then how does the soul appear to be happy or unhappy? By reflection. Just as if a piece of pure crystal be put on a table and a red flower be put near it, the crystal appears to be red, so all these appearances of happiness or unhappiness are but reflections; the soul itself has no sort of colouring. The soul is separate from nature; nature is one thing, soul another, eternally separate. The *Sânkhyas* say that intelligence is a compound, that it grows and wanes, that it changes, just as the body changes, and that its nature is nearly the same as that of the body. As a finger-nail is to the body, so is body to intelligence. The nail is a part of the body, but it can be pared off hundreds of times, and the body will still last. Similarly, the intelligence lasts æons, while this body can be pared off, thrown off. Yet intelligence cannot be immortal, because it changes — growing and waning. Anything that changes cannot be immortal. Certainly intelligence is manufactured, and that very fact shows us that there must be something beyond that, because it cannot be free. Everything connected with matter is in nature, and therefore bound for ever. Who is free? That free one must certainly be beyond cause and effect. If you say that the idea of freedom is a delusion, I will say that the idea of bondage is also a delusion. Two facts come into our consciousness, and stand or fall by each other. One is that we are bound. If we want to go through a wall, and our head bumps against that wall, we are limited by that wall. At the same time we find will, and think we can direct our will everywhere. At every step these contradictory ideas are coming to us. We have to believe that we are free, yet at every moment we find we are not free. If one idea is a delusion, the other is also a delusion, and if one is true, the other also is true, because both stand upon the same basis — consciousness. The *Yogî* says both are true; that we are bound so far as intelligence goes, that we are free as far as the soul is concerned. It is the real nature of man, the Soul, the *Puruṣa*, which is beyond all law of causation. Its freedom is percolating through layers and layers of matter, in various forms of intelligence, and mind, and all these things. It is its light which is shining through all. Intelligence has no light of its own. Each organ has a particular centre in the brain; it is not that all the organs have one centre; each organ is separate. Why do all these perceptions harmonize, and where do they get their unity? If it were in the brain there would be one centre only for the eyes, the nose, the ears, while we know for certain that there are different centres for each. But a man can see and hear at the same time, so a unity must be back of intelligence. Intelligence is eternally connected with the brain, but behind even intelligence stands the *Puruṣa*, the unit, where all these different sensations and perceptions join and become one. Soul itself is the centre where all the different organs converge and become unified, and that Soul is free, and it is its freedom that tells you every moment that you are free. But you mistake, and mingle that freedom every moment with intelligence and mind. You try to attribute that freedom to the intelligence, and immediately find that intelligence is not free; you attribute that freedom to the body, and immediately nature tells you that you are again mistaken. That is why there is this mingled sense of freedom and bondage at the same time. The

Yogī analyses both what is free and what is bound, and his ignorance vanishes. He finds that the *Puruṣa* is free, is the essence of that knowledge which, coming through the *Buddhi*, becomes intelligence, and, as such, is bound.

21. The nature of the experienced is for him.

Nature has no light of its own. As long as the *Puruṣa* is present in it, it appears light, but the light is borrowed; just as the moon's light is reflected. All the manifestations of nature are caused by this nature itself, according to the *Yogīs*; but nature has no purpose in view, except to free the *Puruṣa*.

22. Though destroyed for him whose goal has been gained, yet is not destroyed, being common to others.

The whole idea of this nature is to make the Soul know that it is entirely separate from nature, and when the Soul knows this, nature has no more attractions for it. But the whole of nature vanishes only for that man who has become free. There will always remain an infinite number of others, for whom nature will go on working.

23. Junction is the cause of the realisation of the nature of both the powers, the experienced and its Lord.

According to this aphorism, when this Soul comes into conjunction with nature, both the power of the

Soul and the power of nature become manifest in this conjunction, and all these manifestations are thrown out. Ignorance is the cause of this conjunction. We see every day that the cause of our pain or pleasure is always our joining ourselves with the body. If I were perfectly certain that I am not this body, I should take no notice of heat and cold, or anything of the kind. This body is a combination. It is only a fiction to say that I have one body, you another, and the sun another. The whole universe is one ocean of matter, and you are the name of a little particle, and I of another, and the sun of another. We know that this matter is continuously changing, what is forming the sun one day, the next day may form the matter of our bodies.

24. Ignorance is its cause.

Through ignorance we have joined ourselves with a particular body, and thus opened ourselves to misery. This idea of body is a simple superstition. It is superstition that makes us happy or unhappy. It is superstition caused by ignorance that makes us feel heat and cold, pain and pleasure. It is our business to rise above this superstition, and the *Yogî* shows us how we can do this. It has been demonstrated that, under certain mental conditions, a man may be burned, yet, while that condition lasts, he will feel no pain. The difficulty is that this sudden upheaval of the mind comes like a whirlwind one minute, and goes away the next. If, however, we attain it scientifically, through

Yoga, we shall permanently attain to that separation of Self from the body.

25. There being absence of that (ignorance) there is absence of junction, which is the thing-to-be-avoided; that is the independence of the seer.

According to this *Yoga* philosophy it is through ignorance that the Soul has been joined with nature and the idea is to get rid of nature's control over us. That is the goal of all religions. Each Soul is potentially divine. The goal is to manifest this Divinity within, by controlling nature, external and internal. Do this either by work, or worship, or psychic control, or philosophy, by one, or more, or all of these—and be free. This is the whole of religion. Doctrines, or dogmas, or rituals, or books, or temples, or forms, are but secondary details. The *Yogí* tries to reach this goal through psychic control. Until we can free ourselves from nature we are slaves; as she dictates so we must go. The *Yogí* claims that he who controls mind controls matter also. The internal nature is much higher than the external, and much more difficult to grapple with, much more difficult to control; therefore he who has conquered the internal nature controls the whole universe; it becomes his servant. *Rája Yoga* propounds the methods of gaining this control. Higher forces than we know in physical nature will have to be subdued. This body is just the external crust of the mind. They are not two different things; they are just as the oyster and its shell. They are but two aspects of one thing; the internal substance of the oyster is taking up matter from outside, and manufacturing the shell. In the same way these internal fine forces which are called mind take up gross matter from outside, and from that manufacture this external shell, or body. If then, we have control of the internal, it is very easy to have control of the external. Then again, these forces are not different. It is not that some forces are physical, and some mental; the physical forces are but the gross manifestations of the fine forces, just as the physical world is but the gross manifestation of the fine world.

26. The means of destruction of ignorance is unbroken practice of discrimination.

This is the real goal of practice — discrimination between the real and the unreal, knowing that the *Puruṣa* is not nature, that it is neither matter nor mind, and that because it is not nature, it cannot possibly change. It is only nature which changes, combining, and recombining, dissolving continually. When through constant practice we begin to discriminate, ignorance will vanish, and the *Puruṣa* will begin to shine in its real nature, omniscient, omnipotent, omnipresent.

27. His knowledge is of the sevenfold highest ground.

When this knowledge comes, it will come, as it were, in seven grades, one after the other, and when one of these has begun we may know that we are getting knowledge. The first to appear will be that we have known what is to be known. The mind will cease to be dissatisfied. While we are aware of thirsting after knowledge we begin to seek here and there, wherever we think we can get some truth, and, failing to find it we become dissatisfied and seek in a fresh direction. All search is vain, until we begin to perceive that knowledge is within ourselves, that no one can help us, that we must help ourselves. When we begin to practise the power of discrimination, the first sign that we are getting near truth will be that that dissatisfied state will vanish. We shall feel quite sure that we have found the truth, and that it cannot be anything else but the truth. Then we may know that the sun is rising, that the morning is breaking for us, and, taking courage, we must persevere until the goal is reached. The second grade will be that all pains will be gone. It will be impossible for anything in the universe, physical, mental, or spiritual, to give us pain. The third will be that we shall get full knowledge, that omniscience will be ours. Next will come what is called freedom of the *Chitta*. We shall realise that all these difficulties and struggles have fallen off from us. All these vacillations of the mind, when the mind cannot be controlled, have fallen down, just as a stone rolls from the mountain top into the valley and never comes up again. The next will be that this *Chitta* itself will realise that it melts away into its causes whenever we so desire. Lastly we shall find that we are established

12

in our Self, that we have been alone throughout the universe, neither body nor mind was ever connected with us, much less joined to us. They were working their own way, and we, through ignorance, joined ourselves to them. But we have been alone, omnipotent, omnipresent, ever blessed; our own Self was so pure and perfect that we required none else. We required none else to make us happy, for we are happiness itself. We shall find that this knowledge does not depend on anything else; throughout the universe there can be nothing that will not become effulgent before our knowledge. This will be the last state, and the *Yogî* will become peaceful and calm, never to feel any more pain, never to be again deluded, never to touch misery. He knows he is ever blessed, ever perfect, almighty.

28. By the practice of the different parts of Yoga the impurities being destroyed knowledge becomes effulgent, up to discrimination.

Now comes the practical knowledge. What we have just been speaking about is much higher. It is away above our heads, but it is the ideal. It is first necessary to obtain physical and mental control. Then the realisation will become steady in that ideal. The ideal being known, what remains is to practise the method of reaching it.

29. Yama, Niyama, Âsana, Prânâyâma, Pratyâhâra, Dhâranâ, Dhyâna, Samâdhi, are the limbs of Yoga.

30. Non-killing, truthfulness, non-stealing, continence, and non-receiving, are called Yama.

A man who wants to be a perfect *Yogî* must give up the sex idea. The Soul has no sex; why should it degrade itself with sex ideas? Later on we shall understand better why these ideas must be given up. Receiving is just as bad as stealing; receiving gifts from others. Whoever receives gifts, his mind is acted on by the mind of the giver, so that the man who receives gifts becomes degenerated. Receiving gifts destroys the independence of the mind, and makes us mere slaves. Therefore, receive nothing.

31. These, unbroken by time, place, purpose, and caste, are (universal) great vows.

These practices, non-killing, non-stealing, chastity, and non-receiving, are to be practised by every man, woman and child, by every soul, irrespective of nation, country or position.

32. Internal and external purification, contentment, mortification, study, and worship of God, are the Niyamas.

External purification is keeping the body pure; a dirty man will never be a *Yogî*. There must be internal purification also. That is obtained by the first-named virtues. Of course internal purity is of greater value than external, but both are necessary, and external purity, without internal, is of no good.

33. To obstruct thoughts which are inimical to Yoga contrary thoughts will be brought.

That is the way to practise all these virtues that have been stated, by holding thoughts of an opposite character in the mind. When the idea of stealing comes, non-stealing should be thought of. When the idea of receiving gifts comes, replace it by a contrary thought.

34. The obstructions to Yoga are killing, etc., whether committed, caused, or approved; either through avarice, or anger, or ignorance; whether slight, middling, or great, and result in innumerable ignorances and miseries. This is (the method of) thinking the contrary.

If I tell a lie, or cause another to tell a lie, or approve of another doing so, it is equally sinful. If it is a very mild lie, still it is a lie. Every vicious thought will rebound, every thought of hatred which you may have thought, in a cave even, is stored up, and will one day come back to you with tremendous power in the form of some misery here. If you project all sorts of hatred and jealousy, they will rebound on you with compound interest. No power can avert them; when once you have put them in motion you will have to bear them. Remembering this, will prevent you from doing wicked things.

35. Non-killing being established, in his presence all enmities cease (in others).

If a man gets the ideal of non-injuring others, before him even animals which are by their nature ferocious will become peaceful. The tiger and the lamb will play together before that *Yogî* and will not hurt each other. When you have come to that state, then alone you will understand that you have become firmly established in non-injuring.

36. By the establishment of truthfulness the Yogi gets the power of attaining for himself and others the fruits of work without the works.

When this power of truth will be established with you, then even in dream you will never tell an untruth, in thought, word or deed; whatever you say will be truth. You may say to a man "Be blessed," and that man will be blessed. If a man is diseased, and you say to him, "Be thou cured," he will be cured immediately.

37. By the establishment of non-stealing all wealth comes to the Yogi.

The more you fly from nature the more she follows you, and if you do not care for her at all she becomes your slave.

38. By the establishment of continence energy is gained.

The chaste brain has tremendous energy, gigantic will power, without that there can be no mental strength. All men of gigantic brains are very continent. It gives wonderful control over mankind. Leaders of men have been very continent, and this is what gave them power. Therefore the *Yogî* must be continent.

39. When he is fixed in non-receiving he gets the memory of past life.

When the *Yogî* does not receive presents from others he does not become beholden to others, but becomes independent and free, and his mind becomes pure, because with every gift he receives all the evils of the giver, and they come and lay coating after coating on his mind, until it is hidden under all sorts of coverings of evil. If he does not receive the mind becomes pure, and the first thing it gets is memory of past life. Then alone the *Yogî* becomes perfectly fixed in his ideal, because he sees that he has been coming and going so many times, and he becomes determined that this time he will be free, that he will no more come and go, and be the slave of Nature.

40. Internal and external cleanliness being established, arises disgust for one's own body, and non-intercourse with other bodies.

When there is real purification of the body, external and internal, there arises neglect of the body, and all this idea of keeping it nice will vanish. What others call the most beautiful face to the *Yogî* will appear to be an animal's face, if there is not intelligence behind it. What the world will call a very common face he will call heavenly, if that spirit shines behind it. This thirst after body is the great bane of human life. So, when this purity is established, the first sign will be that you do not care to think you are a body. It is only when purity comes that we get rid of the body idea.

41. There also arises purification of the Sattva, cheerfulness of the mind, concentration, conquest of the organs, and fitness for the realisation of the Self.

By this practice the *Sattva* material will prevail, and the mind will become concentrated and cheerful. The first sign that you are becoming religious is that you are becoming cheerful. When a man is gloomy that may be dyspepsia, but it is not religion. A pleasurable feeling is the nature of the *Sattva*. Everything is pleasurable to the *Sâttvika* man, and when this comes, know that you are progressing in *Yoga*. All pain is caused by *Tamas*, so you must get rid of that; moroseness is one of the results of *Tamas*. The strong, the well-knit, the young, the healthy, the daring alone are fit to be *Yogîs*. To the *Yogî* everything is bliss, every human face that he sees brings cheerfulness to him. That is the sign of a virtuous man. Misery is casued by sin, and by no other cause. What business have you with clouded faces; it is terrible. If you have a clouded face do not go out that day, shut yourself up in your room. What right have you to carry this disease out into the world? When your mind has become controlled you will have control over the whole body; instead of being a slave to this machine, the machine will be your slave. Instead of this machine being able to drag the soul down it will be its greatest helpmate.

42. From contentment comes superlative happiness.

43. The result of mortification is bringing powers to the organs and the body, by destroying the impurity.

The results of mortification are seen immediately sometimes by heightened powers of vision, and so on, hearing things at a distance, etc.

44. By repetition of the mantram comes the realisation of the intended deity.

The higher the beings that you want to get the harder is the practice.

45. By sacrificing all to Iswara comes Samâdhi.

By resignation to the Lord, *Samâdhi* becomes perfect.

46. Posture is that which is firm and pleasant.

Now comes *Âsana*, posture. Until you can get a firm seat you cannot practise the breathing and other exercises. The seat being firm means that you do not feel the body at all; then alone it has become firm. But, in the ordinary way, you will find that as soon as you sit for a few minutes all sorts of disturbances come into the body; but when you have got beyond the idea of a concrete body you will lose all sense of the body. You will feel neither pleasure nor pain. And when you take your body up again it will feel so rested; it is the only perfect rest that you can give to the body. When you have succeeded in conquering the body and keeping it firm, your practice will remain firm, but while you are disturbed by the body your nerves become disturbed, and you cannot concentrate the mind. We can make the seat firm by thinking of the infinite. We cannot think of the Absolute Infinite, but we can think of the infinite sky.

47. By slight effort and meditating on the unlimited (posture becomes firm and pleasant).

Light and darkness, pleasure and pain, will not then disturb you.

48. Seat being conquered, the dualities do not obstruct.

The dualties are good and bad, heat and cold, and all the pairs of opposites.

49. Controlling the motion of the exhalation and the inhalation follows after this.

When the posture has been conquered, then this motion is to be broken and controlled, and thus we come to *Prâṇâyâma;* the controlling of the vital forces of the body. *Prâṇa* is not breath, though it is usually so translated. It is the sum-total of the cosmic energy. It is the energy that is in each body, and its most apparent manifestation is the motion of the lungs. This motion is caused by *Prâṇa* drawing in the breath, and is what we seek to control in *Prâṇâyâma*. We begin by controlling the breath, as the easiest way of getting control of the *Prâṇa*.

50. Its modifications are either external or internal, or motionless, regulated by place, time, and number, either long or short.

The three sorts of motion of this *Prâṇâyâma* are, one by which we draw the breath in, another by which we throw it out, and the third action is when the breath is held in the lungs, or stopped from entering the lungs. These, again, are varied by place and time. By place is meant that the *Prâṇa* is held to some particular part of the body. By time is meant how long the *Prâṇa* should be confined to a certain place, and so we are told how many seconds to keep one motion, and how many seconds to keep another. The result of this *Prâṇâyâma* is *Udghâta*, awakening the *Kuṇḍalinî*.

51. The fourth is restraining the Prâṇa by directing it either to the external or internal objects.

This is the fourth sort of *Prâṇâyâma*. *Prâṇa* can be directed either inside or outside.

52. From that, the covering to the light of the Chitta is attenuated.

The *Chitta* has, by its own nature, all knowledge. It is made of *Sattva* particles, but is covered by *Rajas* and *Tamas* particles, and by *Prâṇâyâma* this coverng is removed.

53. The mind becomes fit for Dhâraṇâ.

After this covering has been removed we are able to concentrate the mind.

54. The drawing in of the organs is by their giving up their own objects and taking the form of the mind-stuff.

These organs are separate states of the mind-stuff. I see a book; the form is not in the book, it is in the mind. Something is outside which calls that form up. The real form is in the *Chitta*. These organs are identifying themselves with, and taking the forms of whatever comes to them. If you can restrain the mind-stuff from taking these forms the mind will remain calm. This is called *Pratyâhâra*. Thence arises supreme control of the organs.

When the *Yogî* has succeeded in preventing the organs from taking the forms of external objects, and in making them remain one with the mind-stuff, then comes perfect control of the organs, and when the organs are perfectly under control, every muscle and nerve will be under control, because the organs are the centres of all the sensations, and of all actions. These organs are divided into organs of work and organs of sensation. When the organs are controlled, the *Yogî* can control all feeling and doing; the whole of the body will be under his control. Then alone one begins to feel joy in being born; then one can truthfully say, "Blessed am I that I was born." When that control of the organs is obtained, we feel how wonderful this body really is.

CHAPTER III.

THE CHAPTER OF POWERS.

We have now come to the chapter which is called the Chapter of Powers.

1. Dhâraṇâ is holding the mind on to some particular object.

Dhâraṇâ (concentration) is when the mind holds on to some object, either in the body, or outside the body, and keeps itself in that state.

2. An unbroken flow of knowledge in that object is Dhyâna.

The mind tries to think of one object, to hold itself to one particular spot, as the top of the head, the heart, etc., and if the mind succeeds in receiving the sensations only through that part of the body, and through no other part, that would be *Dhâraṇâ*, and when the mind succeeds in keeping itself in that state for some time it is called *Dhyâna* (meditation).

3. When that, giving up all forms, reflects only the meaning, it is Samâdhi.

That is, when in meditation all forms are given up. Suppose I were meditating on a book, and that I have gradually succeeded in concentrating the mind on it, and perceiving only the internal sensations, the meaning, unexpressed in any form, that state of *Dhyâna* is called *Samâdhi*.

4. (These) three (when practised) in regard to one object is Samyama.

When a man can direct his mind to any particular object and fix it there, and then keep it there for a long time, separating the object from the internal part, this is *Samyama;* or *Dhâraṇâ*, *Dhyâna*, and *Samâdhi*, one following the other, and making one. The form of the thing has vanished, and only its meaning remains in the mind.

5. By the conquest of that comes light of knowledge.

When one has succeeded in making this *Samyama*, all powers come under his control. This is the great instrument of the *Yogî*. The objects of knowledge are infinite, and they are divided into the gross, grosser, grossest, and the fine, finer, finest, and so on. This *Samyama* should be first applied to gross things, and when you begin to get knowledge of the gross, slowly, by stages, it should be brought to finer things.

6. That should be employed in stages.

This is a note of warning not to attempt to go too fast.

7. These three are nearer than those that precede.

Before these we had the *Prâṇâyâma*, the *Âsana*, the *Yama* and *Niyama;* these are external parts of these three — *Dhâranâ*, *Dhyâna*, and *Samâdhi*. Yet these latter even are external to the seedless *Samâdhi*. When a man has attained to them he may attain to omniscience and omnipotence, but that would not be salvation. These three would not make the mind *Nirvikalpa*, changeless, but would leave the seeds for getting bodies again, only when the seeds are, as the *Yogî* says, "fried," do they lose the possibility of producing further plants. These powers cannot fry the seed.

8. But even they are external to the seedless (Samâdhi),

Compared with that seedless *Samâdhi*, therefore, even these are external. We have not yet reached the real *Samâdhi*, the highest, but to a lower stage, in which this universe still exists as we see it, and in which are all these powers.

9. By the suppression of the disturbed modifications of the mind, and by the rise of modifications of control, the mind is said to attain the controlling modifications—following the controlling powers of the mind.

That is to say, in this first state of *Samâdhi*, the modifications of the mind have been controlled, but not perfectly, because if they were, there would be no modifications. If there is a modification which impels the mind to rush out through the senses, and the *Yogî* tries to control it, that very control itself will be a modification. One wave will be checked by another wave, so it will not be real *Samâdhi*, when all the waves have subsided, as control itself will be a wave. Yet this lower *Samâdhi* is very much nearer to the higher *Samâdhi* than when the mind comes bubbling out.

10. Its flow becomes steady by habit.

The flow of this continuous control of the mind becomes steady when practised day after day and the mind obtains the faculty of constant concentration.

11. Taking in all sorts of objects, and concentrating upon one object, these two powers being destroyed and manifested respectively, the Chitta gets the modification called Samâdhi.

The mind is taking up various objects, running into all sorts of things and then there is a higher state of the mind, when it takes up one object and excludes all others. *Samâdhi* is the result of that.

12. The one-pointedness of the Chitta is when it grasps in one, the past and present.

How are we to know that the mind has become concentrated? Because time will vanish. The more time vanishes the more concentrated we are. In common life we see that when we are interested in a book we do not note the time at all, and when we leave the book we are often surprised to find how many hours have passed. All time will have the tendency to come and stand in the one present. So the definition is given, when the past and present come and stand in one, the more concentrated the mind.

13. By this is explained the threefold transformations of form, time and state, in fine or gross matter, and in the organs.

By this the threefold changes in the mind-stuff as to form, time, and state, are explained. The mind-stuff is changing into *Vṛittis*, this is change as to form. To be able to hold the changes to the present time is change as to time. To be able to make the mind-stuff go to the past forms giving up the present even, is change as to state. The concentrations taught in the preceding aphorisms were to give the *Yogí* a voluntary control over the transformations of his mind-stuff which alone will enable him to make the *Samyama* before named.

14. That which is acted upon by transformations, either past, present or yet to be manifested, is the qualified.

That is to say, the qualified is the substance which is being acted upon by time and by the *Samskâras*, and getting changed and being manifested all the time.

15. The succession of changes is the cause of manifold evolution.

16. By making Samyama on the three sorts of changes comes the knowledge of past and future.

We must not lose sight of the first definition of *Samyama*. When the mind has attained to that state when it identifies itself with the internal impression of the object, leaving the external, and when, by long practice, that is retained by the mind, and the mind can get into that state in a moment, that is *Samyama*. If a man in that state wants to know the past and future he has to make a *Samyama* on the changes in the *Samskâras*. Some are working now at present, some have worked out, and some are waiting to work; so by making a *Samyama* on these he knows the past and future.

17. By making Samyama on word, meaning, and knowledge, which are ordinarily confused, comes the knowledge of all animal sounds.

The word represents the external cause, the meaning represents the internal vibration that travels to the brain through the channels of the *Indriyas*, conveying the external impression to the mind, and knowledge represents the reaction of the mind, with which comes perception. These three confused, make our sense objects. Suppose I hear a word; there is first the external vibration, next the internal sensation carried to the mind by the organ of hearing, then the mind reacts, and I know the word. The word I know is a mixture of the three, vibration, sensation, and reaction. Ordinarily these three are inseparable; but by practice the *Yogî* can separate them. When a man has attained to this, if he makes a *Samyama* on any sound, he understands the meaning which that sound was intended to express, whether it was made by man or by any other animal.

18. By perceiving the impressions, knowledge of past life.

Each experience that we have comes in the form of a wave in the *Chitta*, and this subsides and becomes finer and finer, but is never lost. It remains there in minute form, and if we can bring this wave up again, it becomes memory. So, if the *Yogî* can make a *Samyama* on these past impressions in the mind, he will begin to remember all his past lives.

19. By making Samyama on the signs in another's body knowledge of that mind comes.

Suppose each man has particular signs on his body, which differentiate him from others; when the *Yogî* makes a *Samyama* on these signs peculiar to a certain man he knows the nature of the mind of that person.

20. But not its contents, that not being the object of the Samyama.

He would not know the contents of the mind by making a *Samyama* on the body. There would be required a twofold *Samyama*, first on the signs in the body, and then on the mind itself. The *Yogî* would then know everything that is in that mind, past, present, and future.

21. By making Samyama on the form of the body the power of perceiving forms being obstructed, the power of manifestation in the eye being separated, the Yogî's body becomes unseen.

A *Yogî* standing in the midst of this room can apparently vanish. He does not really vanish, but he will not be seen by anyone. The form and the body are, as it were, separated. You must remember that this can only be done when the *Yogî* has attained to that power of concentration when form and the thing formed have been separated. Then he makes a *Samyama* on that, and the power to perceive forms is obstructed, because the power of perceiving forms comes from the junction of form and the thing formed. By this the disappearance or concealment of words which are being spoken is also explained.

22. Karma is of two kinds, soon to be fructified, and late to be fructified. By making Samyama on that, or by the signs called Arisṭha, portents, the Yogîs know the exact time of separation from their bodies.

When the *Yogî* makes a *Samyama* on his own *Karma*, upon those impressions in his mind which are now working, and those which are just waiting to work, he knows exactly by those that are waiting when his body will fall. He knows when he will die, at what hour, even at what minute. The Hindûs think very much of that knowledge or consciousness of the nearness of death, because it is taught in the *Gîtâ* that the thoughts at the moment of departure are great powers in determining the next life.

23. By making Samyama on friendship, etc., various strength comes.

24. By making Samyama on the strength of the elephant, etc., that strength comes to the Yogi.

When a *Yogî* has attained to this *Samyama* and wants strength, he makes a *Samyama* on the strength of the elephant, and gets it. Infinite energy is at the disposal of everyone, if he only knows how to get it. The *Yogî* has discovered the science of getting it.

25. By making Samyama on that effulgent light comes the knowledge of the fine, the obstructed, and the remote.

When the *Yogî* makes *Samyama* on that effulgent light in the heart he sees things which are very remote, things, for instance, that are happening in a distant place, and which are obstructed by mountain barriers and also things which are very fine.

26. By making Samyama on the sun the knowledge of the world.

27. On the moon the knowledge of the cluster of stars.

28. On the pole star the motions of the stars.

29. On the navel circle the knowledge of the constitution of the body.

30. On the well of the throat cessation of hunger.

When a man is very hungry, if he can make *Samyama* on the pit of the throat hunger ceases.

31. On the nerve called Kurma fixity of the body.

When he is practising the body is not disturbed.

32. On the light from the top of the head sight of the Siddhas.

The *Siddhas* are beings who are a little above ghosts. When the *Yogî* concentrates his mind on the top of his head he will see these *Siddhas*. The word *Siddha* does not refer to those men who have become free — a sense in which it is often used.

33. Or by the power of Pratibhâ all knowledge.

All these can come without any *Samyama* to the man who has the power of *Pratibhâ* (enlightenment from purity). This is when a man has risen to a high state of *Pratibhâ;* then he has that great light. All things are apparent to him. Everything comes to him naturally, without making *Samyama* or anything.

34. In the heart, knowledge of minds.

35. Enjoyment comes by the non-discrimination of the very distant soul and Sattva. Its actions

are for another: Samyama on this gives knowledge of the Puruṣa.

This power of non-attachment acquired through purity gives the *Yogî* the enlightenment called *Pratibhâ*.

36. From that arises the knowledge of hearing, touching, seeing, tasting, and smelling, belonging to Pratibhâ.

37. These are obstacles to Samâdhi; but they are powers in the worldly state.

If the *Yogî* knows all these enjoyments of the world it comes by the junction of the *Puruṣa* and the mind. If he wants to make *Samyama* on this, that they are two different things, nature and soul, he gets knowledge of the *Puruṣa*. From that arises discrimination. When he has got that discrimination he gets the *Pratibhâ*, the light of supreme genius. These powers, however, are obstructions to the attainment of the highest goal, the knowledge of the pure Self, and freedom; these are, as it were, to be met in the way, and, if the *Yogî* rejects them, he attains the highest. If he is tempted to acquire these, his farther progress is barred.

38. When the cause of bondage has become loosened, the Yogi, by his knowledge of manifestation through the organs, enters another's body.

The *Yogî* can enter a dead body, and make it get up and move, even while he himself is working in another body. Or he can enter a living body, and hold that man's mind and organs in check, and for the time being act through the body of that man. That is done by the *Yogî* coming to this discrimination of *Puruṣa* and nature. If he wants to enter another's body he makes a *Samyama* on that body and enters it, because, not only is his Soul omnipresent, but his mind also, according to the *Yogî*. It is one bit of the universal mind. Now, however, it can only work through the nerve currents in this body, but when the *Yogî* has loosened himself from these nerve currents, he will be able to work through other things.

39. By conquering the current called Udâna the Yogî does not sink in water, or in swamps, and he can walk on thorns.

Udâna is the name of the nerve current that governs the lungs, and all the upper parts of the body, and when he is master of it he becomes light in weight. He cannot sink in water; he can walk on thorns and sword blades, and stand in fire, and so on.

40. By the conquest of the current Samâna he is surrounded by blaze.

Whenever he likes light flashes from his body.

41. By making Samyama on the relation between the ear and the Âkâsa comes divine hearing.

There is the *Âkâśa*, the ether, and the instrument, the ear. By making *Samyama* on them the *Yogî* gets divine hearing; he hears everything. Anything spoken or sounded miles away he can hear.

42. By making Samyama on the relation between the Akâśa and the body the Yogi becoming light as cotton wool goes through the skies.

This *Âkâśa* is the material of this body; it is only *Âkâśa* in a certain form that has become the body. If the *Yogî* makes a *Samyama* on this *Âkâśa* material of his body, it acquires the lightness of *Âkâśa*, and can go anywhere through the air.

43. By making Samyama on the real modifications of the mind, which are outside, called great disembodiedness, comes disappearance of the covering to light.

The mind in its foolishness thinks that it is working in this body. Why should I be bound by one system of nerves, and put the Ego only in one body, if the mind is omnipresent? There is no reason why I should. The *Yogî* wants to feel the Ego wherever he likes. When he has succeeded in that all covering to light goes away, and all darkness and ignorance vanish. Everything appears to him to be full of knowledge.

44. By making Samyama on the elements, beginning with the gross, and ending with the superfine, comes mastery of the elements.

The *Yogî* makes *Samyama* on the elements, first on the gross, and then on the finer states. This *Samyama* is taken up more by a sect of the Buddhists. They take a lump of clay, and make *Samyama* on that, and gradually they begin to see the fine materials of which it is composed, and when they have known all the fine materials in it, they get power over that element. So with all the elements, the *Yogî* can conquer them all.

45. From that comes minuteness, etc., glorification of the body, and indestructibleness of the bodily qualities.

This means that the *Yogî* has attained the eight powers. He can make himself as light as a particle, he can make himself huge, as heavy as the earth, or as light as the air; he will rule everything he wants, he will conquer everything he wants, a lion will sit at his feet like a lamb, and all his desires be fulfilled at will.

46. The glorification of the body are beauty, complexion, strength, adamantine hardness.

The body becomes indestructible; fire cannot injure it. Nothing can injure it. Nothing can destroy it until the *Yogî* wishes. "Breaking the rod of time he lives in this universe with his body." In the *Vedas* it is written that for that man there is no more disease, death or pain.

47. By making Samyama on the objectivity, knowledge and egoism of the organs, by gradation comes the conquest of the organs.

In perception of external objects the organs leave their place in the mind and go towards the object; that is followed by knowledge and egoism. When the *Yogî* makes *Samyama* on these by gradation he conquers the organs. Take up anything that you see or feel, a book, for instance, and first concentrate the mind on the thing itself. Then on the knowledge that is in the form of a book, and then the Ego that sees the book. By that practice all the organs will be conquered.

48. From that comes glorified mind, power of the organs independently of the body, and conquest of nature.

Just as by the conquest of the elements comes glorified body, so from the conquest of the mind will come glorified mind.

49. By making Samyama on the Sattva, to him who has discriminated between the intellect and the Puruśa come omnipresence and omniscience.

When we have conquered nature, and realised the difference between the *Puruśa* and nature, that the *Puruśa* is indestructible, pure and perfect, when the *Yogî* has realised this, then comes omnipotence and omniscience.

50. By giving up even these comes the destruction of the very seed of evil; he attains Kaivalya.

He attains aloneness, independence. Then that man is free. When he gives up even the ideas of omnipotence and omniscience, there will be entire rejection of enjoyment, of the temptations from celestial beings. When the *Yogî* has seen all these wonderful powers, and rejected them, he reaches the goal. What are all these powers? Simply manifestations. They are no better than dreams. Even omnipotence is a dream. It depends on the mind. So long as there is a mind it can be understood, but the goal is beyond even the mind.

51. There should be entire rejection of enjoyment of the temptations from celestial beings, for fear of evil again.

There are other dangers too; gods and other beings come to tempt the *Yogî*. They do not want anyone to be perfectly free. They are jealous, just as we are, and worse than we sometimes. They are very much afraid of losing their places. Those *Yogîs* who do not reach perfection die and become gods; leaving the direct road they go into one of the side streets, and get these powers. Then again they have to be born; but he who is strong enough to withstand these temptations, and go straight to the goal, becomes free.

52. By making Samyama on a particle of time and its multiples comes discrimination.

How are we to avoid all these things, these *Devas*, and heavens, and powers? By discrimination, by knowing good from evil. Therefore a *Samyama* is given by which the power of discrimination can be strengthened. This is by making a *Samyama* on a particle of time.

53. Those which cannot be differentiated by species, sign and place, even they will be discriminated by the above Samyama.

The misery that we suffer comes from ignorance, from non-discrimination between the real and the unreal. We are all taking that which is bad for that which is good, and that which is a dream for that which is real. Soul is the only reality, and we have forgotten it. Body is an unreal dream, and we think we are all bodies. So this non-discrimination is the cause of misery, and it is caused by ignorance. When discrimination comes it brings strength, and then alone can we avoid all these various ideas of body, and heavens, and gods and *Devas*. This ignorance arises through differentiating by species, sign or place. For instance, take a cow. The cow is differentiated from the dog, as species. Even with the cows alone how do we make the distinction between one cow and another? By signs. If two objects are exactly similar they can be distinguished if they are in different places. When objects are so mixed up that even these differentiæ will not help us, the power of discrimination acquired by the above-mentioned practice will give us the ability to distinguish them. The highest philosophy of the *Yogî* is based upon this fact, that the *Puruṣa* is pure and perfect, and is the only simple that exists in this universe. The body and mind are compounds, and yet we are ever identifying ourselves with them. That is the great mistake that the distinction has been lost. When this power of discrimination has been attained, man sees that everything in this world, mental and physical, is a compound, and, as such, cannot be the *Puruṣa.*

54. The saving knowledge is that knowledge of discrimination which covers all objects, all means.

Isolation, that is the goal; when that is attained, the soul will find that it was alone all the time, and it required no one to make it happy. As long as we require someone else to make us happy we are slaves. When the *Puruṣa* finds that It is free, and does not require anything to complete Itself, that this nature is quite unnecessary, then freedom is attained. Then comes this *Kaivalya.*

55. By the similarity of purity between the Sattva and the Puruṣa comes Kaivalya.

When the soul realises that it depends on nothing in the universe, from gods to the lowest atom, that is called *Kaivalya* (isolation) and perfection. It is attained when this mixture of purity and impurity called mind has been made as pure as the *Puruṣa* Itself; then the *Sattva*, the mind, reflects only the unqualified essence of purity, which is the *Puruṣa.*

CHAPTER IV.

INDEPENDENCE.

1. The Siddhis (powers) are attained by birth, chemical means, power of words, mortification or concentration.

SOMETIMES a man is born with the *Siddhis*, powers, of course from the exercise of powers he had in his previous birth. In this birth he is born, as it were, to enjoy the fruits of them. It is said of *Kapila*, the great father of the *Sânkhya* Philosophy, that he was a born *Siddha*, which means, literally, a man who has attained to success. The *Yogîs* claim that these powers can be gained by chemical means. All of you know that chemistry originally began as alchemy; men went in search of the philosopher's stone, and elixirs of life, and so forth. In India there was a sect called the *Râsâyanas*. Their idea was that ideality, knowledge, spirituality and religion, were all very right, but that the body was the only instrument by which to attain to all these. If the body broke now and then it would take so much more time to attain to the goal. For instance, a man wants to practise *Yoga*, or wants to become spiritual. Before he has advanced very far he dies. Then he takes another body and begins again, then dies, and so on, and in this way much time will be lost in dying and being born again. If the body could be made strong and perfect, so that it would get rid of birth and death, we should have so much more time to become spiritual. So these *Râsâyanas* say, first make the body very strong, and they claim that this body can be made immortal. Their idea is that if the mind is manufacturing the body, and if it be true that each mind is only one particular outlet to that infinite energy, and that there is no limit to each particular outlet getting any amount of power from outside, why is it impossible that we should keep our bodies all the time? We shall have to manufacture all the bodies that we shall ever have. As soon as this body dies we shall have to manufacture another. If we can do that why cannot we do it just here and now, without getting out? The theory is perfectly correct. If it is possible that we live after death, and make other bodies, why is it impossible that we should have the power of making bodies here, without entirely dissolving this body, simply changing it continually? They also thought that in mercury and in sulphur was hidden the most wonderful power, and that by certain preparations of these a man could keep the body as long as he liked. Others believed that certain drugs could bring powers, such as flying through the air, etc. Many of the most wonderful medicines of the present day we owe to the *Râsâyanas*, notably the use of metals in medicine. Certain sects of *Yogîs* claim that many of their principal teachers are still living in their old bodies. *Patanjali*, the great authority on *Yoga*, does not deny this. The power of words There are certain sacred words called *Mantrams*, which have power, when repeated under proper conditions, to produce these extraordinary powers We are living in the midst of such a mass of miracles, day and night, that we do not think anything of them. There is no limit to man's power, the power of words and the power of mind. Mortification. You find that in every religion mortifications and asceticisms have been practised. In these religious conceptions the Hindûs always go to the extremes. You will find men standing with their hands up all their lives, until their hands wither and die. Men sleep standing, day and night, until their feet swell, and, if they live, the legs become so stiff in this position that they can no more bend them, but have tc stand all their lives. I once saw a man who had raised his hands in this way, and I asked him how it felt when he did it first. He said it was awful torture. It was such torture that he had to go to a river and put himself in water, and that allayed the pain for a little. After a month he did not suffer much. Through such practices powers (*Siddhis*) can be attained. Concentration. The concentration is *Samâdhi*, and that is *Yoga* proper; that is the principal theme of this science, and it is the highest means. The preceding ones are only secondary, and we cannot attain to the highest through them. *Samâdhi* is the means through which we can gain anything and everything, mental, moral or spiritual.

2. The change into another species is by the filling in of nature.

Patanjali has advanced the proposition that these powers come by birth, sometimes by chemical means, or they may be got by mortification and he has admitted that this body can be kept for any length of time. Now he goes on to state what is the cause of the change of the body into another species, which he says is by the filling in of nature. In the next aphorism he will explain this.

3. Good deeds, etc., are not the direct causes in the transformations of nature, but they act as breakers of obstacles to the evolutions of nature, as a farmer breaks the obstacles to the course of water, which then runs down by its own nature.

When a farmer is irrigating his field the water is already in the canals, only there are gates which keep the water in. The farmer opens these gates, and the water flows in by itself, by the law of gravitation. So, all human progress and power are already in everything; this perfection is every man's nature, only it is barred in and prevented from taking its proper course. If anyone can take the bar off in rushes nature. Then the man attains the powers which are his already. Those we called wicked become saints, as soon as the bar is broken and nature rushes in. It is nature that is driving us towards perfection, and eventually she will bring everyone there. All these practices and struggles to become religious are only negative work, to take off the bars, and open the doors to that perfection which is our birthright, our nature. To-day the evolution theory of the ancient *Yogîs* will be better understood in the light of modern research. And yet the theory of the *Yogîs* is a better explanation. The two causes of evolution advanced by the moderns, *viz.*, sexual selection and survival of the fittest, are inadequate. Suppose human knowledge to have advanced so much as to eliminate competition, both from the function of acquiring physical sustenance and of acquiring a mate. Then, according to the moderns, human progress will stop and the race will die. And the result of this theory is to furnish every oppressor with an argument to calm the qualms of conscience, and men are not lacking, who, posing as philosophers, want to kill out all wicked and incompetent persons (they are, of course, the only judges of competency), and thus preserve the human race! But the great ancient evolutionist, *Patanjali*, declares that the true secret of evolution is the manifestation of the perfection which is already in every being; that this perfection has been barred, and the infinite tide behind is struggling to express itself. These struggles and competitions are but the results of our ignorance, because we do not know the proper way to unlock the gate and let the water in. This infinite tide behind must express itself, and it is the cause of all manifestation, not competition for life, or sex gratification, which are only momentary, unnecessary, extraneous effects, caused by ignorance. Even when all competition has ceased this perfect nature behind will make us go forward until every one has become perfect. Therefore there is no reason to believe that competition is necessary to progress. In the animal the man was suppressed, but, as soon as the door was opened, out rushed man. So, in man there is the potential god, kept in by the locks and bars of ignorance. When knowledge breaks these bars the god becomes manifest.

4. From egoism alone proceed the created minds.

The theory of *Karma* is that we suffer for our good or bad deeds, and the whole scope of philosophy is to approach the glory of man. All the Scriptures sing the glory of man, of the soul, and then, with the same breath, they preach this *Karma*. A good deed brings such a result, and a bad deed such a result, but, if the soul can be acted upon by a good or a bad deed it amounts to nothing. Bad deeds put a bar to the manifestation of our nature, of the *Puruṣa*, and good deeds take the obstacles off, and its glory becomes manifest. But the *Puruṣa* itself is never changed. Whatever you do never destroys your own glory, your own nature, because the soul cannot be acted upon by anything, only a veil is spread before it, hiding its perfection.

5. Though the activities of the different created minds are various, the one original mind is the controller of them all.

These different minds, which will act in these different bodies, are called made-minds, and the bodies made-bodies; that is, manufactured bodies and minds. Matter and mind are like two inexhaustible storehouses. When you have become a *Yogi* you have learned the secret of their control. It was yours all the time, but you had forgotten it. When you become a *Yogí* you recollect it. Then you can do anything with it, manipulate it in every way you like. The material out of which that manufactured mind is created is the very same material which is used as the macrocosm. It is not that mind is one thing and matter another, but they are different existences of the same thing. *Asmitâ*, egoism, is the material, the fine state of existence out of which these made-minds and made-bodies of the *Yogí* will be manufactured. Therefore, when the *Yogí* has found the secret of these energies of nature he can manufacture any number of bodies, or minds, but they will all be manufactured out of the substance known as egoism.

6. Among the various Chittas that which is attained by Samâdhi is desireless.

Among all the various minds that we see in various men, only that mind which has attained to *Samâdhi*, perfect concentration, is the highest. A man who has attained certain powers through medicines, or through words, or through mortifications, still has desires, but that man who has attained to *Samâdhi* through concentration is alone free from all desires.

7. Works are neither black nor white for the Yogis; for others they are threefold, black, white, and mixed.

When the *Yogî* has attained to that state of perfection, the actions of that man, and the *Karma* produced by those actions, will not bind him, because he did not desire them. He just works on; he works to do good, and he does good, but does not care for the result, and it will not come to him. But for ordinary men, who have not attained to that highest state, works are of three kinds, black (evil actions), white (good actions), and mixed.

8. From these threefold works are manifested in each state only those desires (which are) fitting to that state alone. (The others are held in abeyance for the time being.)

Suppose I have made the three kinds of *Karma*, good, bad and mixed, and suppose I die and become a god in heaven; the desires in a god body are not the same as the desires in a human body. The god body neither eats nor drinks; what becomes of my past unworked *Karmas*, which produce as their effect the desire to eat and drink ? Where would these *Karmas* go when I became a god ? The answer is that desires can only manifest themselves in proper environments. Only those desires will come out for which the environment is fitted; the rest will remain stored up. In this life we have many godly desires, many human desires, many animal desires. If I take a god body, only the good desires will come up, because for them the environments are suitable. And if I take an animal body, only the animal desires will come up, and the good desires will wait. What does that show ? That by means of environment we can check these desires. Only that *Karma* which is suited to and fitted for the environments will come out. This proves that the power of environment is the great check to control even *Karma* itself.

9. There is consecutiveness in desire, even though separated by species, space and time, there being identification of memory and impressions.

Experiences becoming fine become impressions; impressions revivified become memory. The word memory here includes unconscious co-ordination of past experience, reduced to impressions, with present conscious action. In each body the group of impressions acquired in a similar body only will become the cause of action in that body. The experiences of dissimilar bodies will be held in abeyance. Each body will act as if it were a descendant of a series of bodies of that species only; thus, consecutiveness of desires will not be broken.

10. Thirst for happiness being eternal desires are without beginning.

All experience is preceded by desire for becoming happy. There was no beginning of experience, as each fresh experience is built upon the tendency generated by past experience; therefore desire is without beginning.

11. Being held together by cause, effect, support, and objects, in the absence of these is its absence.

These desires are held together by cause and effect; if a desire has been raised it does not die without producing its effect. Then again, the mind-stuff is the great storehouse, the support of all past desires, reduced to *Samskâra* form; until they have worked themselves out they will not die. Moreover, so long as the senses receive the external objects fresh desires will arise. If it be possible to get rid of these, then alone desires will vanish.

12. The past and future exist in their own nature, qualities having different ways.

13. They are manifested or fine, being of the nature of the Guṇas.

The *Guṇas* are the three substances, *Sattva*, *Rajas*, and *Tamas*, whose gross state is the sensible universe. Past and future arise from the different modes of manifestation of these *Guṇas*.

14. The unity in things is from the unity in changes. Though there are three substances their changes being co-ordinated all objects have their unity.

15. The object being the same, perception and desire vary according to the various minds.

16. Things are known or unknown to the mind, being dependent on the colouring which they give to the mind.

17. The states of the mind are always known because the lord of the mind is unchangeable.

The whole gist of this theory is that the universe is both mental and material. And both the mental and material worlds are in a continuous state of flux. What is this book ? It is a combination of molecules in constant change. One lot is going out, and another coming in; it is a whirlpool, but what makes the unity ? What makes it the same book ? The changes are rhythmical; in harmonious order they are sending impressions to my mind, and these pieced together make a continuous picture, although the parts are continuously changing. Mind itself is continuously changing. The mind and body are like two layers in the same substance, moving at different rates of speed. Relatively, one being slower and the other quicker, we can distinguish between the two motions. For instance, a train is moving, and another carriage is moving slowly alongside it. It is possible to find the motion of both these, to a certain extent. But still something else is necessary. Motion can only be perceived when there is something else which is not moving. But when two or three things are relatively moving, we first perceive the motion of the faster one, and then that of the slower ones. How is the mind to perceive ? It is also in a flux. Therefore another thing is necessary which moves more slowly, then you must get to something in which the motion is still slower, and so on, and you will find no end. Therefore logic compels you to stop somewhere. You must complete the series by knowing something which never changes. Behind this never ending chain of motion is the *Puruṣa*, the changeless, the colourless, the pure. All these impressions are merely reflected upon it, as rays of light from a camera are reflected upon a white sheet, painting hundreds of pictures on it, without in any way tarnishing the sheet.

18. Mind is not self-luminous, being an object.

Tremendous power is manifested everywhere in nature, but yet something tells us that it is not self-luminous, not essentially intelligent. The *Puruṣa* alone is self-luminous, and gives its light to everything. It is its power that is percolating through all matter and force.

19. From its being unable to cognise two things at the same time.

If the mind were self-luminous it would be able to cognise everything at the same time, which it cannot. If you pay deep attention to one thing you lose another. If the mind were self-luminous there would be no limit to the impressions it could receive. The *Puruṣa* can cognise all in one moment; therefore the *Puruṣa* is self-luminous, and the mind is not.

20. Another cognising mind being assumed there will be no end to such assumptions and confusion of memory.

Let us suppose there is another mind which cognises the first, there will have to be something which cognises that, and so there will be no end to it. It will result in confusion of memory, there will be no storehouse of memory.

21. The essence of knowledge (the Puruṣa) being unchangeable, when the mind takes its form, it becomes conscious.

Patanjali says this to make it more clear that knowledge is not a quality of the *Puruṣa*. When the mind comes near the *Puruṣa* it is reflected, as it were, upon the mind, and the mind, for the time being, becomes knowing and seems as if it were itself the *Puruṣa*.

22. Coloured by the seer and the seen the mind is able to understand everything.

On the one side the external world, the seen, is being reflected, and on the other, the seer is being reflected; thus comes the power of all knowledge to the mind.

23. The mind through its innumerable desires acts for another (the Puruṣa), being combinations.

The mind is a compound of various things, and therefore it cannot work for itself. Everything that is a combination in this world has some object for that combination, some third thing for which this combination is going on. So this combination of the mind is for the *Puruṣa*.

24. For the discriminating the perception of the mind as Âtman ceases.

Through discrimination the *Yogî* knows that the *Puruṣa* is not mind.

25. Then bent on discriminating the mind attains the previous state of Kaivalya (isolation).

Thus the practice of *Yoga* leads to discriminating power, to clearness of vision. The veil drops from the eyes, and we see things as they are. We find that this nature is a compound, and is showing the panorama for the *Puruṣa*, who is the witness; that this nature is not the Lord, that the whole of these combinations of nature are simply for the sake of showing these phenomena to the *Puruṣa*, the enthroned king within. When discrimination comes by long practice fear ceases, and the mind attains isolation.

26. The thoughts that arise as obstructions to that are from impressions.

All the various ideas that arise making us believe that we require something external to make us happy are obstructions to that perfection. The *Puruṣa* is happiness and blessedness by its own nature. But that knowledge is covered over by past impressions. These impressions have to work themselves out.

27. Their destruction is in the same manner as of ignorance, etc., as said before.

28. Even when arriving at the right discriminating knowledge of the essences, he who gives up the fruits, unto him comes as the result of perfect discrimination, the Samâdhi called the cloud of virtue.

When the *Yogî* has attained to this discrimination, all these powers will come that were mentioned in the last chapter, but the true *Yogî* rejects them all. Unto him comes a peculiar knowledge, a particular light called the *Dharma Megha*, the cloud of virtue. All the great prophets of the world whom history has recorded had this. They had found the whole foundation of knowledge within themselves. Truth to them had become real. Peace and calmness, and perfect purity became their own nature, after they had given up all these vanities of powers.

29. From that comes cessation of pains and works.

When that cloud of virtue has come, then no more is there fear of falling, nothing can drag the *Yogî* down. No more will there be evils for him. No more pains.

30. Then knowledge, bereft of covering and impurities, becoming infinite, the knowable becomes small.

Knowledge itself is there; its covering is gone. One of the Buddhistic scriptures sums up what is meant by the Buddha (which is the name of a state). It defines it as infinite knowledge, infinite as the sky. Jesus attained to that and became the Christ. All of you will attain to that state, and knowledge becoming infinite, the knowable becomes small. This whole universe, with all its knowable, becomes as nothing before the *Puruṣa*. The ordinary man thinks himself very small, because to him the knowable seems to be so infinite.

31. Then are finished the successive transformations of the qualities, they having attained the end.

Then all these various transformations of the qualities, which change from species to species, cease for ever.

32. The changes that exist in relation to moments, and which are perceived at the other end (at the end of a series) are succession.

Patanjali here defines the word succession, the changes that exist in relation to moments. While I am thinking, many moments pass, and with each moment there is a change of idea, but we only perceive these changes at the end of a series. So, perception of time is always in the memory. This is called succession, but for the mind that has realised omnipresence all these have finished. Everything has become present for it; the present alone exists, the past and future are lost. This stands controlled, and all knowledge is there in one second. Everything is known like a flash.

33. The resolution in the inverse order of the qualities, bereft of any motive of action for the Puruṣa, is Kaivalya, or it is the establishment of the power of knowledge in its own nature.

Nature's task is done, this unselfish task which our sweet nurse Nature had imposed upon herself. As it were, she gently took the self-forgetting soul by the hand, and showed him all the experiences in the universe, all manifestations, bringing him higher and higher through various bodies, till his glory came back, and he remembered his own nature. Then the kind mother went back the same way she came, for others who also have lost their way in the trackless desert of life. And thus is she working, without beginning and without end. And thus through pleasure and pain, through good and evil, the infinite river of souls is flowing into the ocean of perfection, of self-realisation.

Glory unto those who have realised their own nature; may their blessings be on us all.

APPENDIX.

References to Yoga.

Śvetâśvatara Upanishad.

Chapter II.

2-6-14. Where the fire is churned, where the air is controlled, where the flow of *Soma* becomes plentiful there a (perfect) mind is created. . . . . Placing the body in which the chest, the throat, and the head are held erect, in a straight posture, making the organs enter the mind, the sage crosses all the fearful currents by means of the raft of *Brahman.*

The man of well regulated endeavours controls the *Prâṇa*, and when it has become quieted breathes out through the nostrils. The persevering sage holds his mind as a charioteer holds the restive horses.

In lonely places, as mountain caves, etc., where the floor is even, free of pebbles or sand, where there are no disturbing noises from men or waterfalls, in places helpful to the mind and pleasing to the eyes, *Yoga* is to be practised (mind is to be joined).

Like snowfall, smoke, sun, wind, fire, firefly, lightning, crystal, moon, these forms, coming before, gradually manifest the *Brahman* in *Yoga*.

When the perceptions of *Yoga*, arising from earth, water, light, fire, ether, have taken place, then *Yoga* has begun. Unto him does not come disease, nor old age, nor death, who has got a body made up of the fire of *Yoga*.

The first signs of entering *Yoga* are lightness, health, the skin becomes smooth, the complexion clear, the voice beautiful, and there is an agreeable odour in the body.

14. As gold or silver, first covered with earth, etc., and then burned and washed, shines full of light, so the embodied man seeing the truth of the *Âtman* as one, attains the goal and becomes sorrowless.

Yâjnavalkya, quoted by Śankara.

" After practising the postures as desired, according to rules, then, O *Gârgî*, the man who has conquered the posture will practise *Prâṇâyâma*.

" On the seat of earth, spreading the *Kuśa* grass, and over it a skin, worshipping *Ganapati* with fruits and sweetmeats, seated on that seat, placing the opposite hands on the knees, holding the throat and head in the same line, the lips closed and firm, facing the east or the north, the eyes fixed on the tip of the nose, avoiding too much food or fasting, the *Nâdis* should be purified according to the above-mentioned rule, without which the practice will be fruitless, thinking of the (seed-word) *Hum*, at the junction of *Pingalâ* and *Iḍâ* (the right and the left nostrils), the *Iḍâ* should be filled with external air in twelve *Mâtrâs* (seconds), then the *Yogî* meditates fire in the same place and the word '*Rang*,' and while meditating thus, slowly rejects the air through the *Pingalâ* (right nostril). Again filling in through the *Pingalâ* the air should be slowly rejected through the *Iḍâ*, in the same way. This should be practised for three or four years, or three or four months, according to the directions of a *Guru*, in secret (alone in a room) in the early morning, at midday, in the evening, and at midnight (until) the nerves become purified, and these are the signs; lightness of body, clear complexion, good appetite, hearing of the *Nâda*. Then should be practised *Prâṇâyâma*, composed of *Rechaka* (exhalation), *Kumbhaka* (retention), and *Pûraka* (inhalation). Joining the *Prâṇa* with the *Apâna* is *Prâṇâyâma*.

"In sixteen *Mâtrâs* filling the body from the head to the feet in thirty-two *Mâtrâs* to be thrown out, with sixty-four the *Kumbhaka* should be made.

"There is another sort of *Prâṇâyâma* in which, with sixteen *Mâtrâs*, the body is to be filled, then the *Kumbhaka* is made with sixty-four, and with thirty-two it should be rejected.

"By *Prâṇâyâma* impurities of the body are thrown out; by *Dhâraṇâ* the impurities of the mind; by *Pratyâhâra* impurities of attachment, and by *Samâdhi* is taken off everything that hides the lordship of the Soul."

Sânkhya.

Book III.

29. By the achievement of meditation, there are to the pure one (the *Puruṣa*) all powers like nature.

30. Meditation is the removal of attachment.

31. It is perfected by the suppression of the modifications.

32 By meditation, posture and performance of one's duties, it is perfected.

33. Restraint of the *Prâṇa* is by means of expulsion and retention.

34. Posture is that which is steady and easy.

36. Also by non-attachment and practice.

75. By practising the discrimination of the principles of nature from the *Puruṣa*, and by giving them up as " not It, not It," discrimination is perfected.

Book IV.

3. Repetition, instruction is to be repeated.

5. As the hawk becomes unhappy if the food is taken away from him, and happy if he gives it up himself (so he who gives up everything voluntarily is happy).

6. As the snake is happy in giving up his old skin.

8. That which is not a means of liberation is not to be thought of; it becomes a cause of bondage, as in the case of *Bharata*.

9. From the association of many things there is obstruction to meditation, through passion, etc., like the shell bracelets on the virgin's hand.

10. It is the same, even in the case of two.

11. The hopeless are happy, like the girl *Pingalâ*.

13. Although devotion is to be given to many institutes and teachers, the essence is to be taken from them all, as the bee takes the essence from many flowers.

14. One whose mind has become concentrated like the arrowmaker's, his meditation is not disturbed.

15. Through transgression of the original rules there is non-attainment of the goal, as in other worldly things.

19. By continence, reverence, and devotion to *Guru*, success comes after a long time (as in the case of *Indra*.)

20. There is no law as to time (as in the case of *Vâmadeva*).

24. Or through association with one who has attained perfection.

27. Not by enjoyments is desire appeased.

Book V.

128. The *Siddhis* attained by *Yoga* are not to be denied.

Book VI.

24. Any posture which is easy and steady is an *Âsana;* there is no other rule.

Vyâsa Sûtra.

Chapter IV., Section 1.

7. Worship is possible in a sitting posture.

8. Because of meditation.

9. Because the meditating (person) is compared to the immovable earth.

10. Also because the *Smritis* say so.

11. There is no law of place; wherever the mind is concentrated, there worship should be performed.

These several extracts give an idea of what other systems of Indian Philosophy have to say upon Yoga.

GLOSSARY

A FEW SIMPLE HELPS TO PRONUNCIATION

â like *a* in f*a*r;
a almost like *u* in b*u*t;
e like *a* in n*a*me;
î like *ee* in s*ee*;
û like *oo* in t*oo*;
ś like *sh* in *sh*ip;
ch like *ch* in ri*ch*;
ai like *i* in f*i*ne.

No attempt is made to give the finer distinctions of Sanskrit pronunciation, as a thorough knowledge of the language would be needed to grasp them.

In this glossary are to be found words commonly used in books and pamphlets on Vedânta, as well as those that are employed in this volume.

GLOSSARY

Abhaya .... Fearlessness.
Abhâva .... Bereft of quality.
Abheda .... Non-separateness; sameness; without distinction.
Abhidhyâ .... Not coveting others' goods, not thinking vain thoughts, not brooding over injuries received from others.
Abhighâta .... Impediment.
Abhimâna .... Pride.
Abhinivêsa .... Attachment to life.
Abhyâsa .... Practice.
Âchârya .... Great spiritual teacher.
Âdarsa .... A mirror—a term sometimes used to denote the finer power of vision developed by the *Yogî*.
Âdhidaivika .... Supernatural.
Adhikâri .... One qualified as a seeker of wisdom.
Aditi .... The infinite, the goddess of the sky.
Âditya .... The Sun.
Âdityas .... Twelve planetary spirits.

Adharma .... Absence of virtue; unrighteousness.

Adrogha .... Not injuring.

Adrogha-Vâk .... One who does not harm others even by words.

Advaita .... (*A-dvaita*) Non-dualism. The monistic system of Vedânta philosophy.

Advaitin .... A follower of *Advaita*.

Adhyâsa .... Reflection, as the crystal reflects the color of the object before it. Superimposition of qualities of one object over another, as of the snake on the rope.

Agni .... The god of fire. Later, the Supreme God of the Vedas.

Aham .... "I."

Aham-Brahmâsmi ...... "I am Brahman."

Ahamkâra .... Egoism. Self-consciousness.

Âhâra .... Gathering in,—as food to support the body or the mind.

Ahimsâ .... Non-injuring in thought, word, or deed.

Ahimsaka .... One who practises *Ahimsâ*.

Âjnâ .... The sixth lotos of the *Yogîs*, corresponding to a nerve-centre in the brain, behind the eyebrows. Divine perception.

Ajnâta................ One who has attained divine wisdom.

Âkâśa................ The all-pervading material of the universe.

Akbar................ Mogul Emperor of India, 1542–1605.

Akhanda.............. Undivided.

Akhanda-Satchidânanda. "The undivided Existence-Knowledge-Bliss Absolute."

Âlambana............. Objective contemplation. The things which are supports to the mind in its travel Godwards.

Amritatvam........... Immortality.

Anâhata.............. lit. "unstruck sound." The fourth lotos of the *Yogîs* in the *Śuśumnâ*, opposite the heart.

Ânanda............... Bliss.

Ananya-Bhakti........ Worship of one particular Deity in preference to all others. In a higher sense, it is seeing all Deities as but so many forms of the One God. Singleness of love and worship.

Anavasâda............ Cheerfulness, not becoming dejected. Strength, both mental and physical.

Animâ .... Attenuation.

Antahkarana .... Internal organ. The mind with its three functions, the cogitative faculty, the determinative faculty and the egoism.

Antaryâmin .... The name of *Iśvara*, —meaning, He who knows everything that is going on within (*antara*) every mind.

Antarârâma........... The *Yogî* who rests in the final contemplation of the Supreme Lord, (*Iśvara*).

Anubhava............. Realization.

Anuddharsa........... Absence of excessive merriment.

Anumâna .... Inference.

Anurakti............. The attachment that comes after the knowledge of the nature of God.

Anurâga.............. Great attachment to *Iśvara.*

Anuvâda.............. A statement referring to something already known.

Apakshiyate .... To decay.

Apânâ................ One of the five manifestations of *prâṇa*. The nerve-current in the body which governs the organs of excretion.

Aparapratyaksha....... Super-sensuous perception.

Aparâvidyâ .... Lower knowledge; knowledge of externals.
Aparigraha .... Non-receiving of gifts; not indulging in luxuries.
Apas .... One of the elements; water; liquid.
Aprâtikûlya .... State of sublime resignation.
Âpta .... One who has attained to realization of God; one who is self-illumined.
Âptavâkyam .... Words of an *Âpta.*
Apura .... Merit.
Âranyakas .... The ancient *Rishis*, dwellers in the forest, also a name given to the books composed by them.
Ariṣtha .... Portents or signs by which a *Yogî* can foretell the exact time of his death.
Ârjavam .... Straight-forwardness.
Arjuna .... The hero of the *Bhagavad Gîtâ*, to whom Krishna (in the form of a charioteer) taught the great truths of the *Vedânta* Philosophy.
Artha .... Meaning.
Arthavattva .... Fruition.
Arûpa .... (*A-rûpa*) Without form.
Âryâvarta .... The land of the Aryans. The name applied by the Hindus to Northern India.

Asamprajnâta .... The highest super-conscious state.
Âsana .... Position of the body during meditation.
Asat .... Non-being or existence. Opposite of *Sat*. Applied to the changing existence of the universe.
Asmitâ .... Non-discrimination.
Aśoka .... A noted Buddhist King, 259–222 B. C.
Âśrama .... Hermitage.
Âsvâda .... lit. "taste,"—applied to the finer faculty of taste developed by the *Yogî*.
Asteyam .... Non-stealing.
Asti .... To be, or exist.
Atharva Veda .... That portion of the *Veda* which treats of psychic powers.
Athâto Brahma-jijnâśâ .. "Then therefore, the enquiry into *Brahman*." [*Vedânta Sutra*, 1–1–I.]
Atikrânta-Chavaniya ... The stage of meditation which ends with what is called "Cloud (or Showerer) of Virtue" *Samâdhi*.
Atithi .... A guest.
Âtman .... The Eternal Self.
Âvarana .... Coverings (of the mind).
Avatâra .... A divine Incarnation.

Avidyâ................ Ignorance.

Âvritti-rasakrit-upadeśât "Repetition (of the mental functions of knowing, meditating, etc., is required) on account of the text giving instructions more than once." [*Vedânta Sutra*, 1–1–IV.]

Avyaktam............. Indiscrete; undifferentiated. Stage of nature, when there is no manifestation.

Bâhya-Bhakti......... External devotion (as worship through rites, symbols, ceremonials, etc., of God).

Bandha .... Bondage.

Banyan-Tree.......... (*Ficus Indica*) Indian fig tree; the branches drop roots to the ground, which grow and form new trunks.

Bhagavad-Gîtâ........ "The Holy Song." A gem of Indian literature containing the essence of the *Vedânta* Philosophy.

Bhagavân............. lit. "Possessor of all powers." A title meaning Great Lord.

Bhagavân Râmakṛishṇa. A great Hindu prophet and teacher of the 19th century, 1835–1886. [See "Life and Sayings of *Śrî Râmakṛishṇa*" by F. Max Müller. London, 1898. Longmans, Green & Co., and Charles Scribner's Sons. New York.]

Bhâgavata-Purâna ..... One of the principal *Purâṇas.*
Bhakta .... A great lover of God.
Bhakti .... Intense love for God.
Bhakti-Yoga .... Union with the Divine through devotion.
Bharata .... A great *Yogî* who suffered much from his excessive attachment to a deer which he brought up as a pet.
Bhâshya .... A commentary.
Bhautika .... Pertaining to the *Bhûtas*, or elements.
Bhâvanâ .... Pondering; meditation.
Bheda .... Separateness.
Bhikshu .... A religious mendicant, a term now usually applied to the Buddhist monks.
Bhoga .... Enjoyment of sense objects.
Bhoja .... The annotator of the Yoga Aphorisms.
Bhûtas .... Gross elements.
Bodha .... Intelligence.
Brahmâ .... The Creator of the universe.
Brahmacharya .... Chastity in thought, word and deed.
Brahmachârin .... One who has devoted himself to continence and the pursuit of spiritual wisdom.
Brahman .... The One Existence, the Absolute.

Brahmaloka........... The world of *Brahmâ*, the highest heaven.

Brâhmaṇa............ A "twice-born man," a Brahmin.

Brâhmaṇas........... Those portions of the Vedas which state the rules for the employment of the hymns at the various ceremonials. Each of the four Vedas has its own *Brâhmaṇa*.

Brahma-Sutra-Bhâshya. Commentary on the aphorisms of *Vedânta*.

Brahmavâdin.......... Teacher of *Brahman*, one who speaks or teaches of *Brahman* or Absolute Being.

Brahmavidyâ.......... Knowledge of *Brahman*, the supreme wisdom that leads to *Mukti*.

Brahmayoga.......... The *Yoga* which leads to the realization of the *Brahman*. (Chap. VIII of the *Bhagavad Gîtâ* is called by that name).

Brahmin.............. An Anglicized form of *Brâhmaṇa*, a member of the *Brâhmaṇa* caste.

Buddha.............. lit. "The Enlightened," the name given to one of the greatest Incarnations recognized by the Hindus, born sixth century B. C.

Buddhi............... The determinative faculty.

Chaitanya............. Pure intelligence. Name of a great Hindu sage (born 1485) who is regarded as a Divine Incarnation.

Chândogya Upanishad... One of the oldest *Upanishads* of the *Sâma-Veda*.

Chârvâka............. A materialist.

Chidâkâśâ......... ... The space of knowledge, where the Soul shines in its own nature.

Chitta................ "Mind-stuff." (The fine material out of which the mind has been manufactured).

Chittâkâśâ............ The mental space.

Dakshinâ............. Offering made to a priest, or teacher, at religious ceremonies.

Dama................. Control of the organs.

Dâna................. Charity.

Dâsya................ "Servantship;" the state of being a devoted servant of God.

Dayâ................. Mercy, compassion, doing good to others without hope of return.

Deha................. Matter, gross body.

Devadatta............ "God-given."

Devas................ The "shining ones," semi-divine beings representing states attained by workers of good.

Devaloka	Abode of the gods.
Devayâna	The path which leads to the sphere of the gods, or the different heavens.
Devî-Bhâgavata	One of the *Purâṇas*, which describes the deeds of the Divine Mother.
Dhâranâ	Holding the mind to one thought for twelve seconds. Concentration.
Dharma	Virtue. Religious duty.
Dharma-megha	"Cloud of virtue," (applied to a kind of *Samâdhi*).
Dhyâna	Meditation.
Dhyânamârga	The way to knowledge through meditation.
Dvandas	Dualities in nature, as heat and cold, pleasure and pain, etc., etc.
Dvesha	Aversion.
Dyâva-Prithivî	Heaven (and) Earth.
Ekâgra	Concentrated state of the mind.
Ekam	One.
Eka-Nisṭhâ	Intense devotion to one chosen ideal.
Ekânta-Bhakti	Singleness of love and devotion to God.

Ekâtma-Vâdam .... Monism. The theory, according to which there is only one intelligent Entıty. Pure idealism.

Ekâyana .... The one stay or support of all things,—hence the Lord.

Ganxpati .... One of the Hindu deities.

Gaṇeśa .... A woman-sage mentioned in the *Upanishads*. She practised *Yoga* and attained to the highest super-conscious state.

Gârgi .... God of wisdom and "remover of obstacles." He is always invoked at the commencement of every important undertaking.

Gauni .... Preparatory stage of *Bhakti-Yoga*.

Gâyatri .... A certain most holy verse of the *Vedas*.

Ghata .... A jar.

Gopîs .... Shepherdesses, worshippers of *Krishna*.

Grahana .... Sense-perception.

Grihastha .... A householder, head of a family.

Gunas .... Qualities, attributes

Guru .... lit. "the dispeller of darkness." A religious teacher who removes the ignorance of the pupil. The real *guru* is a transmitter of the spiritual impulse that quickens the spirit and awakens a genuine thirst for religion.

Hamsa .... The *Jîva*, or individual soul.

Hanumân............. The great *Bhakta* hero of the *Râmâyana.*

Hari................. lit. "One who steals the hearts and reason of all by His beauty," hence the Lord, a name of God.

Haṭha Yoga........... The science of controlling body and mind, but with no spiritual end in view, bodily perfection being the only aim.

Haṭha-Yogî (or *Yogin*).. One who practices "*Haṭha-Yoga.*"

Hiranyagarbha .... lit. "golden wombed." Applied to *Brahmâ*, the Creator, as producing the universe out of Himself.

Hum.................. A mystic word used in meditation as symbolic of the highest Bliss.

Iḍâ.................. The nerve current on the left side of the spinal cord; the left nostril.

Indra	Ruler of the gods.
Indriyâni	Sense organs.
Indriyas	The internal organs of perception.
Iśâna	One of the *devas*.
Ishtam	Chosen ideal (from "*ish*," to wish). That aspect of God which appeals to one most.
Ishta Nisthâ	Devotion to one ideal.
Ishtâpûrta	The works which bring as reward the enjoyments of the heavens.
Iśvara	The Supreme Ruler; the highest possible conception through reason, of the Absolute, which is beyond all thought.
Iśvarapranidhâna	Meditation on *Iśvara*.
Îśvara Pranidhânâdvâ	A *Sûtra* of *Patanjali* — entitled "By worship of the Supreme Lord."
Jada	Inanimate.
Jâgrat	Waking state.
Jâti	Species.
Jâyate	To be born.
Jîva	The individual soul. The one Self as appearing to be separated into different entities; corresponding to the ordinary use of the word "*soul*."

Jîvatman.............. The *Âtman* manifesting as the *Jîva*.

Jîvan Mukta.......... lit. "Living Freedom." One who has attained liberation (*Mukti*) even while in the body.

Jnâna................. Pure intelligence. Knowledge.

Jnâna-chaksu.......... One whose vision has been purified by the realization of the Divine.

Jnânakânda........... The knowledge portion or philosophy of the Vedas.

Jnâna-yajna .... "Wisdom-Sacrifice." Perfect unselfishness, purity and goodness which lead to *Jnâna*, or supreme wisdom (*Moksha*).

Jnânî [or *Jnânin*] ..... One who seeks liberation through pure reason or philosophy.

Kaivalya .... Isolation. Oneness with Absolute Being.

Kâla .... Time.

Kalpa .... A cycle (in evolution).

Kalyâna .... Blessings.

Kâma .... Desire.

Kapila................. Author of the *Sânkhya* Philosophy, and the father of the Hindu Evolutionists.

Kapilavastu .... Birthplace of *Gautama* the *Buddha*.

Kârikâ .... A running commentary.

Karma .... Work or action, also effects of actions; the law of cause and effect in the moral world.

Karmakânda .... The ritualistic portion of the Vedas.

Karmendriyas .... Organs of action.

Karma-Yoga .... Union with the Divine through the unselfish performance of duty.

Khanda .... Differentiated, or divided; division.

Klesa .... Troubles.

Krishna .... An Incarnation of God who appeared in India about 1400 B. C. Most of his teachings are embodied in the *Bhagavad Gîtâ*.

Kriyâ .... Action, ritual, ceremonial.

Kriyamâna .... The *Karma* we are making at present.

Kriyâ-Yoga .... Preliminary *Yoga*, the performance of such acts as lead the mind higher and higher.

Kshana ... . Moments.

Kshatriya .... Member of the warrior (or second) caste of ancient India.

Kshetra .... lit. "the perishable," also "a field." Applied to the human body (as the field of action.)

Kshetrajna............ The knower of *Kshetra*. (Gîtâ, Chap. XII.) The soul.

Kumbhaka............ Retention of the breath in the practice of *prâṇâyâma*.

Kundalini............. lit. "the coiled-up." The residual energy, located according to the *Yogîs*, at the base of the spine, and which in ordinary men produces dreams, imagination, psychical perceptions, etc., and which, when fully aroused and purified, leads to the direct perception of God.

Kuntî................ The mother of the five *Pâṇḍavas*, the heroes who opposed the *Kauravas* at the battle of *Kurukshetra*, the account of which forms the principal theme of the *Mahâbhârata*, the Indian epic.

Kurma............... The name of a nerve upon which the *Yogîs* meditate.

Kurma-Purâna....... One of the eighteen principal *Purânas*.

Kuśa................ A kind of Indian grass used in religious rites.

Madhubhumiba........ The second stage of the *Yogî* when he gets beyond the argumentative condition.

Madhumati .... lit. "honeyed." The state when knowledge gives satisfaction as honey does.

Mathurâ..... .... Sweet. That form of *Bhakti* in which the relation of the devotee towards God is like that of a loving wife to her husband.

Madvâchârya.......... Commentator of the dualistic school of the Vedânta philosophy.

Mahâkâśa .... lit. "Great space" (applied to ordinary space).

Mahâpurusha .... Great Soul. (Incarnation.)

Mahat .... lit. "The great one." Cosmic intelligence.

Mahattattva.......... Great principle. The ocean of intelligence evolved first from indiscrete nature, according to *Sânkhya* philosophy.

Mahâyoga............. Seeing the Self as one with God.

Maitrîya.............. lit. "Full of compassion." The name of a Hindu sage.

Manas................ The deliberative faculty of the mind.

Mantra............... Any prayer, holy verse, sacred or mystic word recited or contemplated during worship.

Mantra-drashtâ .... "Seer of thought." One possessed of super-sensuous knowledge.

Manipûra .... lit. "Filled with jewels." The third lotos of the *Yogîs*, opposite the navel (in the *Śuśumnâ*).

Mâtrâs .... Seconds.

Matha.... .... Monastery.

Mathurâ [Now known as "*Muttra*"]... ... Birth-place of *Kṛishṇa*.

Mâyâ .... Mistaking the unreal and phenomenal for the real and eternal. Commonly translated illusion. (lit. "which baffles all measurement.")

Mîmânsâ .... lit. "Solution of a problem." One of the six schools of Indian philosophy.

Moksha .... Freedom, liberation (*Mukti*).

Moksha-dharma........ The virtues which lead to liberation of the soul.

Mṛityu .... Death. Another name for *Yama*.

Mukti .... Emancipation from rebirth.

Mûlâdhâra............ The basic lotos of the *Yogîs*.

Mumukśutvam .... Desire for liberation.

Mundaka-Upanishad.... One of the twelve principal *Upanishads*.

Muni................. A (religious) sage.

Nâda .... Sound, finer than is heard by our ears.

Nâda-Brahma .... The "sound-*Brahman*." The *Om*, that undifferentiated Word, which has produced all manifestation.

Nâḍi................. A tube along which something flows—as the blood currents, or nervous energies.

Nâḍi-suddhi....... ... lit. "Purification of the channel through which the nerve currents flow." One of the elementary breathing exercises.

Naiśthika............. One possessed of a singleness of devotion towards a high ideal of life.

Namah............... Salutation.

Nâma-rûpa .... Name and form.

Nâmaśakti .... The power of the name of God.

Nàrada............... The great "god-intoxicated" sage of ancient India, who is reputed to have possessed all the "powers" described in *Yoga* philosophy.

Nârada-Sutra......... The Aphorisms of *Nârada* on *Bhakti*.

Nârâyana. .... "Mover on the waters," a title of *Vishnu*.

Natarâja .... lit. "Lord of the stage." Sometimes used for God as the Lord of this vast stage the universe.

"*Neti, Neti*" . ... "Not this, not this."

Nimitta............... Operative cause.

Nirâlambana.......... lit. "Supportless," a very high stage of meditation, according to *Yoga* philosophy.

Nirbija............... lit. "Without seed." The highest form of *Samâdhi* or super-conscious state of the mind according to *Yoga* philosophy.

Nirguna.............. Without attributes or qualities.

Nishkâmakarma .... Unselfish action. To do good acts without caring for the results.

Nitya .... Permanent, eternal.

Nirukta .... Science dealing with etymology and the meaning of words.

Nirvâna .... Freedom; extinction or "blowing out" of delusions.

Nirvichâra .... Without discrimination.

Nirvikalpa............ Changeless.

Nirvitarka............ Without question or reasoning.

Nivritti .... "Revolving away from."

Nishthâ .... Singleness of attachment.

Niyama .... The virtues of cleanliness, contentment, mortification, study and self-surrender.

Nyâya................ The school of Indian logic. The science of logical philosophy.

Ojas .... lit. "The illuminating or bright." The highest form of energy attained by a constant practice of continence and purity.

Om or *Omkâra* .... The most holy word of the *Vedas*. A symbolic word meaning the Supreme Being, the Ocean of Knowledge and Bliss Absolute.

Om tat sat .... lit. "*Om* That Existence." That Ocean of Knowledge and Bliss Absolute, the only Reality.

Pada.................. Foot.

Pâda.................. Chapter.

Parâ.................. Supreme.

Parâ-Bhakti .... Supreme devotion.

Paramahamsa......... Supreme soul.

Parâvidyâ .... Highest knowledge.

Parinamate .... To ripen.

Parjanya. .... God of rain, and of the clouds.

Patanjali............. Founder of the *Yoga* School of Philosophy.

Pingalâ .... The nerve-current on the right side of the spinal cord; also the right nostril.

Pingalâ .... A courtesan who abandoned her vicious life and became remarkable for her piety and virtue.

Pitris .... Forefathers, ancestors.

Pradhâna .... lit. "The chief." The principal element; a name used for nature in *Sânkya* philosophy.

Prajnâ .... Highest knowledge which leads to the realization of the Deity.

Prajnâjyoti .... One who has been illumined with knowledge transcending the senses.

Prakṛiti .... Nature.

Prakṛitilayas .... Souls that have got all the powers that nature has by becoming one with nature.

Prahlâda .... The chief of *Bhaktas.* [Devotees.]

Pramâna .... Means of proof.

Pramêya .... Correct cognition.

Prâṇa .... The sum total of the cosmic energy, the vital forces of the body.

Prâṇâyâma .... Controlling the *prâṇa.*

Pranidhâna	Unceasing devotion.
Prârabdha	The works or *Karma* whose fruits we have begun to reap in this life.
Prasankhyâna	Abstract contemplation.
Prathamakalpika	Argumentative condition of the conscious *Yogî*.
Pratibhâ	Divine illumination.
Pratîka	lit. "Going towards." A finite symbol standing for the infinite *Brahman*.
Pratimâ	The use of images as symbols.
Prativishaya	That which is applied to the different objects, *i. e.*, the organs of sense.
Pratyâhâra	Making the mind introspective.
Pratyagâtman	The internal self; the self-luminous.
Pratyaksham	Direct perception.
Pravritti	"Revolving towards."
Prîti	Pleasure in God.
Prithivî	One of the elements; earth; solids.
Pûraka	Inhalation.
Purâṇas	Writings containing the Hindu mythology.
Puruśa	The Soul.
Pûrva-paksha	The *prima facie* view.

Q'uran .... The Mahommedan Scriptures.

Râga.................. Attachment to those things that please the senses.

Râgânugâ............. The highest form of love and attachment to the Lord.

Râja .... lit. "To shine." Royal.

Râja Hamsa .... Swan.

Rajas .... Activity. One of the three principles which form the essence of nature.

Râja Yoga............ lit. "Royal *yoga*." The science of conquering the internal nature, for the purpose of realizing the Divinity within.

Râkshasa .... A demon.

Râmânuja .... A noted commentator of the *Vishiśtadvaita* School of Philosophy (qualified monistic).

Râma .... An Incarnation of God, and hero of the celebrated epic—the "*Râmâyana*."

Râmâyana .... A celebrated Indian epic poem written by Valmiki, a sage.

Rang.................. A symbolic word for the highest wisdom.

Rasâyanas .... The alchemists of ancient India.

Rechaka .... Exhalation.

Rig-Veda	Oldest portion of the *Vedas*, composed of hymns.
Rishi	lit. "Seer of *mantras*" (thoughts). One possessed of super-sensuous knowledge.
Ritambharâprajna	One whose knowledge is truth-supporting.
Rudra	A name of a Vedic god.
Śabda	Sound.
Śabdabrahma	The creative word corresponding to the *Logos*.
Śabda Nishtham Jagat	"Through sound the world stands."
Sabija Yoga	"Seeded" meditation (that is where all seeds of future *Karma* are not yet destroyed).
Saguna	With qualities.
Saguna-Brahma	The qualified or lower Brahman.
Saguna-vidyâ	Qualified knowledge.
Sahaśrâra	The "thousand-petalled lotos," a figurative expression of the *Yogîs* describing the brain.
Sakhya	Friendship.
Śakti	Power.
Sâlokya	Dwelling in the presence of God.

Sama .... Not allowing the mind to externalize.

Sâma-Veda .... The hymn portion of the *Veda*, or that portion which was sung during the ceremonies.

Samâdhi .... Super-consciousness.

Samâdhâna............ Constant practice.

Samâna .... The nerve current that controls the function of digestion.

Śâmânyatadrishta ...... Inference based on superficial reasoning.

Samâpatti............. lit. "Treasures." Used in *Yoga* philosophy to indicate the different stages of meditation.

Samarasa............. Equality.

Samaṣṭi.............. The universal.

Sâmipya .... Closeness to God.

Samprajnâta........... The first stage of super-consciousness which comes through deep meditation.

Samsâra.............. Endless cycle of manifestation.

Samskâras .... Impressions in the mind-stuff that produce habits.

Samyama .... lit. "Control." In the *Yoga* philosophy it is technically used for that perfect control of the powers of the mind, by which the *Yogî* can know anything in the universe.

Sânandam .... The "blissful *Samâdhi*." The third step of the *samprajnâta samâdhi*. The object of meditation in this state is the "thinking organ" bereft of activity and dullness. (*Rajas* and *Tamas*.)

Sanchita .... The stored up, past *Karma*, whose fruits we are not reaping now, but which we shall have to reap in the future.

Sândilya .... Writer of the Aphorisms of Divine Love (*Bhakti*) from the *Advaita* point of view.

Śankarâchârya .... The great exponent and commentator of the non-dualistic school of Vedânta. He is supposed to have lived in India about the eighth century A. D.

Sânkhya .... lit. "That which reveals truth perfectly." The name of a famous system of Indian philosophy, founded by the great sage Kapila.

Sankocha .... Shrinking, contraction or non-manifestation.

Sannyâsa .... Complete renunciation of all worldly position, property and name.

Sannyâsin .... One who makes *Sannyâsa*, and lives a life of self-sacrifice, devoting himself entirely to religion.

Sânta .... Peaceful or gentle love.

Śânta-Bhakta .... A devotee who has attained to peace through the path of Divine love.

Sântih .... Peace.

Santośa .... Contentment.

Sârupya .... Growing like God.

Śâstra .... Books accepted as Divine authority. Sacred Scriptures.

Sat .... Existence-Absolute.

Satchidânanda .... " Existence–Knowledge–Bliss Absolute."

Sattva .... Illumination material. One of the three principles which form the essence of nature.

Sattva-purshânvatâkhyâti The perception of the Self as different from the principles of nature.

Sâttvika .... Having the *Sattva* quality highly developed, hence one who is pure and holy.

Satyam .... Truthfulness.

Saucham .... Cleanliness.

Savichâra .... With discrimination. (A mode of meditation.)

Savitarka............. Meditation with reasoning or question.

Sâyujya................ Unity with Brahman.

Sâkshi................. Witness.

Siddha-Guru........... A teacher who has attained *Mukti.*

Siddhânta............... Decisive knowledge.

Siddhas................ Semi-divine beings, or *Yogis,* who have attained supernatural powers.

Siddhis................ The supernatural powers which come through the practice of *Yoga.*

Śikshâ................. The science dealing with pronunciation and accents.

Śishya................. A student or disciple of a *Guru.*

Śiva................... The "Destroyer" of the Hindu trinity. Sometimes regarded in the Hindu mythology as the One God.

Śivoham............... "*I am Śiva*" (or eternal bliss).

Śloka.................. Verse.

Smriti................. (1) Memory. (2) Any authoritative religious book, except the *Vedas.*

Soham................. "I am He."

Soma.................. A certain plant, the juice of which was used in the ancient sacrifices.

Sphota .... The eternal, essential material of all ideas or names, which makes words possible, yet is not any definite word in a fully formed state. The inexpressible Manifestor behind all the expressed, sensible universe. The power through which the Lord creates the universe. Its symbol is the eternal *Om*.

Śrâddhâ .... Strong faith in religion.

Śravana .... (1) Hearing, the ears. (2) The finer power of hearing developed by the *Yogî*.

Śrî .... Holy, or blessed.

Śrî Bhâshya .... Name of the qualified non-dualistic commentary of Vedânta by *Râmânuja*.

Śrotiyas .... lit. "High born," or born of a noble family. The Hindu students who know the *Vedas* by heart.

Śruti .... The *Vedas*, so called because transmitted orally from father to son in ancient times. The *Vedas* are regarded by all orthodox Hindus as Divine revelation and as the supreme authority in religious matters.

Sthiti	Stability.
Sthula Śarira	Gross body.
Śukshma Śarira [sometimes called "*Linga Śarira*"]	Fine or subtle body.
Śunya Vâda	Doctrine of the void; nihilism.
Śushupti	Deep, dreamless sleep.
Śushumnâ	The name given by the *Yogîs* to the hollow canal which runs through the centre of the spinal cord.
Sûtra	lit. "Thread." Usually means aphorism.
Svâdhisthâna	lit. "Abode of Self." Second lotos of the *Yogîs*, between base of spine and the navel.
Svâdhyâya	Study.
Svâhâ!	"May it be perpetuated," or "so be it." An expression used in making oblation.
Svapna	The dream state.
Svapneśvara	Commentator of the Aphorisms of *Sândilya*.
Svarûpa	Natural form.
Svasti	A blessing, meaning "Good be unto you."
Svâti	Name of a star.
Svarga	Heaven.
Svâmi	A title meaning "master," or "spiritual teacher."
Śvetâsvatara-Upanishad.	One of the chief *Upanishads* of the *Yajur-Veda*.

Tadîyatâ .... lit. "His-ness." The state when a man has forgotten himself altogether, in his love for the Lord, and does not feel that anything belongs to him personally.

Tamas .... "Darkness," inertia.

Tanmâtras .... Fine materials.

Tantras .... Books held to be sacred by a certain sect in India.

Tantrîkas .... Followers of the *Tantras*.

Tapas .... Controlling the body by fasting or other means. Austerity.

Târaka .... Saviour.

Tarka .... Question or reasoning.

"*Tat tvam asi*" .... "That thou art."

Tattvas .... Categories, principles, truths.

Tejas .... One of the elements; fire; heat.

Titikshâ .... Ideal forbearance. "All-sufferingness."

Trishnâ .... Thirst, desire.

Tulsidâs .... A great sage and poet who popularised the famous epic, the *Râmâyana*, by translating it from Sanskrit into Hindustani dialect.

Turîya .... The fourth, or highest state of consciousness.

Tyâga .... Renunciation.

Udâna .... Nerve current governing the organs of speech, etc.

Uddhârsa............. Excessive merriment.

Udgîtha .... lit. "That which is chanted aloud," hence the *Pranava* or *Om.*

Udgâtha.............. Awakening the *Kundalini.*

Upâdâna .... The material cause of the world.

Upâdhi............... Limiting adjunct.

Uparati .... Not thinking of things of the senses; discontinuing external religious observances.

Upâyapratyaya .... A state of abstract meditation.

Uttara Gîtâ........... The name of a book supposed to be related by *Śri Krishna* for the further instruction of *Arjuna.*

Uttara Mîmânsâ .... . Another name for the *Vedânta* philosophy, written originally in the form of aphorisms by *Vyâsa.*

Vach or *Vâk* .... lit. "speech." The Word, the Logos.

Vâda................. Argumentative knowledge.

Vairâgyam............ Non-attachment to the attractions of the senses. Renunciation.

Vaiśeshika .... A branch of the *Nyâya* school of philosophy; the Atomic school.

Vaishnavas .... The followers or worshippers of *Vishnu*, who form one of the principal Hindu religious sects.

Vâmadeva .... A great *Rishi* who possessed the highest spiritual enlightenment from the time of his birth.

Vânaprastha . ... The forest life. Third of the four stages into which the life of a man was divided in ancient India.

Varâha-Purâna .... One of the eighteen principal *Puraṇas.*

Vardhate .... To grow.

Vârtikam .... A concise explanatory note.

Varuna .... The old Vedic god of the sky.

Vâsanâ .... A habit or tendency arising from an impression remaining unconsciously in the mind from past *Karma.*

Vâsudeva .. .. Manifestation of the highest Being.

Vâtsalya .... The affection of parents for children.

Vâyu. .... lit. "the vibrating." The air.

Vedanâ .... The fine power of feeling developed by the *Yogî*.

Vedas .... The Hindu Scriptures, consisting of the *Rig-Veda*, the *Yajur-Veda*, the *Sama-Veda*, the *Artharva-Veda;* also the *Brahmanas* and the *Upanishads;* comprising the hymns, rituals and philosophy of the Hindu religion.

Vedânta............... The final philosophy of the *Vedas*, as expressed in the *Upanishads*. The philosophical system which embraces all Indian systems of philosophy,—the monistic, the mono-dualistic and the dualistic.

Vêdâvai anantah .... A quotation from the *Vedas*, meaning "The Scriptures are infinite."

Videha .... Disembodied, or unconscious of body.

Vidyâ .... Science, or knowledge.

Vidvân .... One who knows.

Vijnâna .... The higher knowledge.

Vikalpa............... Verbal delusion, doubt, notion, fancy.

Vikaranabhâva .... Uninstrumental perception.

Vikshipta .... A scattered or confused state of the mind.

Vimoksha .... Absence of desire. Absolute freedom.

Vinâ .... A stringed musical instrument of India.

Viparyaya .... False conception of a thing whose real form does not correspond to that conception, as mother of pearl mistaken for silver.

Vipra .... A sage who was born and bred a Brahmin.

Viraha .... Intense misery due to separation from the beloved one.

Virya .... Strength, energy.

Vishnu .... The "Preserver" of the Hindu trinity, who takes care of the universe, and who incarnates from time to time to help mankind.

Viśishtâdvaita .... Qualified non-dualism. A school of Indian philosophy, founded by Râmânuja, a great religious reformer, which teaches that the individual soul is a part of God.

Viśishtâdvaitin......... A follower of the above school of philosophy; a qualified non-dualist.

Viśoka............ ... "Sorrowless."

Vivekânanda .... "Bliss-in-discrimination."

Vitarka .... Questioning or philosophical enquiry.

Viveka .... Discrimination (of the true from the false).

Viśuddha .... The fifth lotos of the *Yogîs*, opposite the throat (in the Sushumnâ).

Vraja .... A suburb of the city of *Muttra*, where *Kṛishṇa* played in his childhood.

Vrindâ .... The attendant of the principal *Gopî*.

Vritti .... lit. "The whirlpool." Wave form in the *chitta;* a modification of the mind.

Vyâna .... The nerve current which circulates all over the body.

Vyâsa .... lit. "One who expands" (as a commentator). One *Vyâsa* was the author of the *Mahâbhârata* and of the *Uttara Mîmânsâ*.

Vyâsa Sutras .... The Vedânta Aphorisms by *Vyâsa*.

Vyaṣṭi .... The particular (as opposed to the universal).

Vyutthâna .... Waking, or returning to consciousness after abstract meditation.

Yajur-Veda .... The ritualistic portion of the *Veda*.

Yama .... The internal purification through moral training, preparatory to *Yoga*. The god of Death, so called from his power of self-control.

Yoga .... Joining; union of the lower self with the higher self, by means of mental control. Any sort of culture that leads us to God.

Yoga Sûtra .... Aphorism on *Yoga*.

Yogî .... One who practices *Yoga*.

Yudhisṭhira .... A great Hindu Emperor who lived about 1400 B. C. He was one of the five *Pâṇḍavas*.

Yuga .... A cycle or age of the world. The present cycle is known in India as the "*Kali-Yuga*" or "Iron-Age."